Books are to be returned on or before
the last date below.

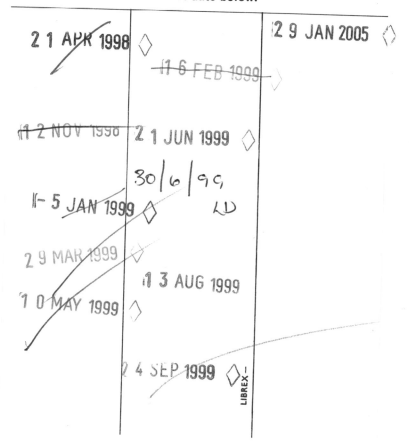

2 1 APR 1998

2 9 JAN 2005

1 6 FEB 1999

1 2 NOV 1998   2 1 JUN 1999

30/6/99
LD

1 - 5 JAN 1999

2 9 MAR 1999

1 3 AUG 1999

1 0 MAY 1999

2 4 SEP 1999

LIBREX

ARCHITECTURE STUDIO

ARCHITECTURE STUDIO

CRANBROOK
ACADEMY OF ART
1986 - 1993

Introduction and project essays by Dan Hoffman

RIZZOLI
NEW YORK

Acknowledgments

The Studio members would like to acknowledge the following for their support in
the making of our work and this book: Roy Slade, president of the Cranbrook
Academy of Art, for his foresight and irrepressible enthusiasm; Agnes Fleckenstein
and the Women's Committee of the Cranbrook Academy for their hard work;
the Swanson family for its contributions in support of architecture at the Academy;
the Cranbrook Academy of Art faculty for their ever-present critique; Sukhwant
Jhaj for his patient observations; and Lilian Bauder, president of the Cranbrook
Educational Community, for her love of architecture and Cranbrook.

First published in the United States of America in 1994 by
Rizzoli International Publications, Inc.
300 Park Avenue South, New York, New York 10010

Library of Congress Cataloging-in-Publication Data
Hoffman, Dan, 1951–
Architecture studio: Cranbrook Academy of Art, 1986–1993 / by Dan Hoffman.
p.   cm.
ISBN 0-8478-1796-2
1. Cranbrook Academy of Art. Dept. of Architecture—Students. 2. Architecture—
Research—Michigan—Bloomfield Hills. 3. Architectural studios—Michigan—
Bloomfield Hills. I. Title.
NA2300.C78H64   1994   93-43292
720—dc20   CIP

Design by Brian Smith
Printed and bound in Singapore

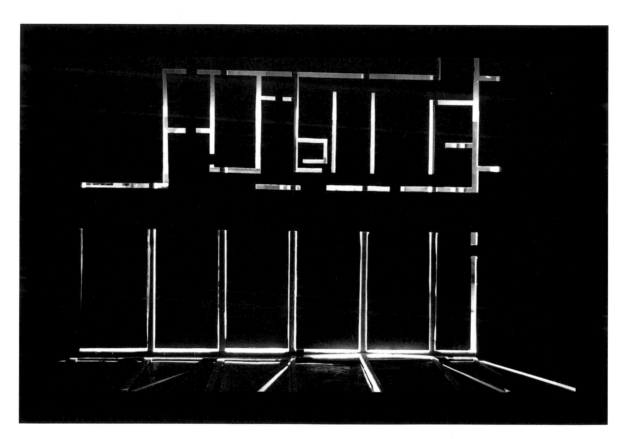

Plan of the Architecture Studio cut into a plywood-faced
stud wall by Adam Womelsdorf

Foreword

The Architecture Studio at Cranbrook Academy of Art, since its beginning under Eliel Saarinen in 1932, has endeavored to extend the understanding of architecture into broader realms. This imperative comes in part from the Studio's presence in a graduate art academy that has always covered a wide range of artistic and craft-based disciplines, an environment in which each discipline is challenged to work at its limit to find areas of common interest and concern. Saarinen encouraged his students to experiment in the various ways of working found at the Academy. The results can be seen in the highly individualistic work of such former graduates as Fumihiko Maki, Harry Weese, Eero Saarinen, Ralph Rapson, Ed Bacon, Ray and Charles Eames, Florence Knoll, and Harry Bertoia, whose work reveals profound respect for crafts and knowledge of the processes of artistic production.

This interest in the relationship between art and craft may be Saarinen's most enduring influence at the Academy. This interest is also reflected in Cranbrook's buildings and grounds, created by Saarinen and others. Though not of a particular school or style, they demonstrate an abiding faith that an intimate contact with the processes and materials of artistic production inevitably leads to beautiful and meaningful work. Since I arrived at Cranbrook in 1977, I have noted that the students and members of the Academy are inspired by the possibilities and demands of *crafting* a work of art or architecture. I have often wondered why this attitude persists at the Academy from year to year, even through artistic tendencies that seem to contradict these very assumptions. The size and relative isolation of the Academy (only 145 students, working at some distance from Detroit) might be one explanation, as might the artist-in-residence studio structure, whereby one working artist, architect, or designer heads each department.

My 1978 appointment of Daniel Libeskind as head of architecture revitalized the department. Libeskind introduced ideas and concepts concerned with deconstructivism in his work and teaching. Through exhibitions, articles, publications, and lectures Libeskind and his students again brought international attention to Cranbrook.

6

Amaranth, 1979–1980 by Michael Hall

Dan Hoffman, who succeeded Libeskind in 1986, has furthered this reputation through his teaching and work. Hoffman, like Libeskind, graduated from the Cooper Union in New York City. He practiced architecture in Detroit, then taught in Canada and Italy before returning to New York to work as a project architect for Edward Larrabee Barnes Associates. Since coming to Cranbrook, Hoffman has been involved in on-site installations, gallery exhibitions of his work, and most recently, a number of building projects at Cranbrook.

Under Hoffman, the Architecture Studio has been influenced by a number of different tendencies and disciplines. The most notable has been the minimalist sculpture of the 1970s and 1980s. Michael Hall, the head of sculpture at the time, brought many major sculptors and their works to the Academy and its grounds. Hall's own work, with its architectural scale and industrial references, was also an important inspiration for the Architecture Studio. Hoffman and his students have extended this concern for industry by considering the effects of its decline on both the culture that it represents and Detroit itself.

The maturity and ambition of the projects in this volume demonstrate the intensity with which work is pursued at Cranbrook. Students are keenly aware of the passion for work that inhabits the walls like a ghost, calling forth a commitment to the traditions of the place, as well as bearing witness to the importance of individual pursuits.

I am pleased to offer this work as part of Cranbrook's ongoing contribution to architecture and the arts.

Roy Slade, President
Cranbrook Academy of Art

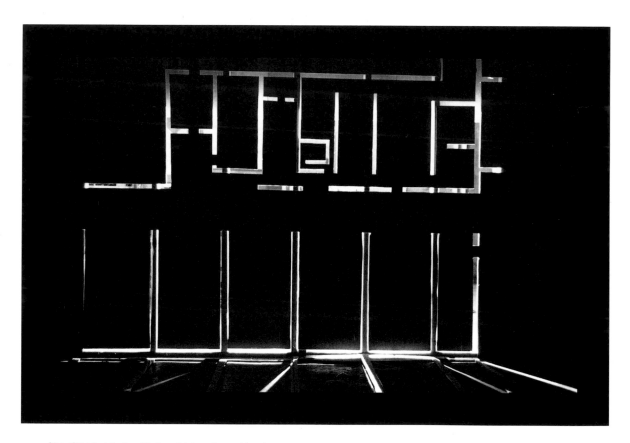

Plan of the Architecture Studio cut into a plywood-faced
stud wall by Adam Womelsdorf

The Third Shadow
Introduction

Michel Serres, in an essay entitled "Mathematics and Philosophy: What Thales Saw," considers the two commentaries on the postulate of similar triangles found in Euclid's *Elements*.[1] These commentaries attribute the first demonstration of the postulate to Greek philosopher Thales, in the context of solving the problem of measuring the height of the great pyramids in Egypt. Thales showed that the height of a pyramid is proportional to the length of the shadow that it casts upon the sand, offering a physical demonstration by placing a stick perpendicular to the ground and noting that the length of its shadow equals the height of the stick when the sun is "halfway up into the sky." The demonstration assumes that the two physical conditions are related by a condition of similarity independent of location and time. Serres observes that the demonstration carries a tacit but critical assumption: "Thales stops time in order to measure space," or time must be sacrificed so that space can come into being.[2] This buried assumption makes geometry possible, for the rule of similarity cannot hold if measurement is a function of the continuous movement of time.

Appropriately, the site of the "sacrifice" is Egypt, a civilization built upon the rhythms of the sun and the cyclical flooding of the Nile. Here time is encoded in ritual, locked in an infinite cycle of days, each with its own cycles of repetitive tasks. The Egyptians could not step out of cyclical time and fix a theoretical point independent of this continuous movement. Indeed, they had no need for the stability of an abstract point that could fix space and manipulate it independently of time. Truth could only be located in the knowledge formed by encoding bodily actions through ritual. Such knowledge could never be fully abstracted since the lived body remains opaque to the rational transparency of the mind. Knowledge was passed on through the shared repetition of bodily acts. The laying of stones, for example, is learned through imitation; one goes over the actions until they are understood by the body as well as by the mind. Perfection is reached through repetition; economy develops through a complex interaction of bodily knowledge and conceptual refinement.

Serres also notes three shadows in Thales's demonstration. The first is the shadow of the stick in the sand, the line stopped momentarily so that a precise, spatial measurement can be made. The second is the shadow on the side of the pyramid, the plane on the surface that differentiates the line from the solid. The third is the shadow within the volume of the pyramid itself, the interior made transparent by the reasoned vision of mind. This recalls Plato's myth of the cave whose inhabitants are chained in such a way that they can only see the movements of their shadows cast by a fire behind them. These unfortunate beings are locked into a time without the illumination offered by a conceptualization of space. All that they can know comes from the play of their shadows on a wall. Plato considers the problem of knowledge by imagining an inhabitant freed from the chains and brought outside to contemplate the brilliant light of the sun, which symbolizes knowledge. (This parallels, in reverse, Thales before the pyramid, moving from the outside in.) The question, then, is how the enlightened inhabitant can instruct the others as to their ignorance. Though Plato does not describe how this might be accomplished, one can assume that it would be through teaching geometry so that the space of the cave and the location of the fire could be understood. Space would again triumph over the darkness of time, and vision would find its true light—not on the surface of things but within the transparent constructions of mind. For the Greeks, to see clearly meant to see through the shadows of appearance to that which is invariant and true.

Once the immobility of space is established, there arises the question of how to explain motion. Aristotle argues in the *Physics* that an object always moves toward "its proper place," which is at rest.[3] Movement is always relative to the nearest immobile surface, which participates in the immobile order of the cosmos. Geometry is also built on the ideas of stability and invariance, allowing the coordination of complex and varied acts of construction, from the precise cutting of stones in a quarry for a distant temple to the explanation and prediction of celestial events. The precision of geometry can be visited over and over again without variation, its constructions experienced today with the freshness that they had thousands of years ago. Geometry establishes the basis of measure, providing the assurance that there exists a point of reference upon which a construction can be made independent of time and place.

The close relationship between architecture and geometry makes questions concerning geometry's origin crucial to architecture. It is therefore important for architects to ask why the myth of geometry's origin is being reconsidered at this time in history. Once the most stable and enduring of all human constructions, architecture virtually symbolized geometry's universal and atemporal qualities, to the extent that classical architectural treatises began with geometry's lessons and derived the orders and organization of buildings from them. The monuments of architecture were considered to be eternal. Even if a building fell into ruin, the endurance of its geometry was not questioned, since its conceptual frame existed outside the material effects of time.

Today we find ourselves swept along in a tide of change that makes us reconsider the endurance and immobility of things. Though it is difficult to isolate any single cause, we must assume that much of the change is driven by advances in technology through the application of scientific concepts to our environment and lives. These concepts begin with the idea that no single spatial or temporal reference point can provide an absolute and fixed orientation. Our knowledge of nature therefore continues to evolve, and we are necessarily tied to this unending process. For example, the ideal conditions of geometry such as the straightness of a line or the flatness of a plane are no longer considered as "givens" with an autonomous existence outside time. They are, rather, conditions of an "idealizing praxis"[4] that views such ideas as endlessly receding limits. Modern technology permits us to make instruments and machines that provoke these conceptual limits through application to specific sites, thereby precipitating the development of new theories and forms of knowledge. These new forms and the instrumental devices of which they are a part are transformed over time, leaving in their wake the history of our attempt to live with and understand their effects.

The subtext of Serres's meditation on the origin of geometry is that we again find ourselves at a transition between one form of knowledge and another. The language of time now challenges that of geometric space. The crucial question, however, is how time can be integrated into our constructions without the relativist view of science dominating. The difficulty is compounded because we still consider time within the confines of a geometric reference, as having beginnings and endings and infinitely divisible quantities. Yet as Bergson points out, time by its nature is not divisible; it is above all a human quality rather than a quantity, an aspect of our memory and the history that memory allows.[5] Time is duration, the sense of passage that moves between and within moments. Time's motion is inescapable; we feel it in all of our actions. Like the third shadow, time is invisible. But unlike Thales's illumination, time must be described in terms of experience rather than reason. The lived moment is the temporal moment, something experienced by the body. The construction of the pyramids in time involved bodily acts performed in the context of temporal cycles, the lifting of one stone upon the other, the movement of the river, the passage of days, and the return of the sun. The pyramid represents the refinement of these acts into a form that provokes the limits of memory. It was left to Thales to find the key that would illuminate the inner structure and reduce its embodied labyrinth to a geometric principle.[6]

Recounting geometry's origin myth also leads us to consider what is about to be lost in the transformation of knowledge. Myths are a form of remembrance, recounting a significant event in human affairs in such a way as to incorporate it into our own, developmental history. In order to be understood a myth must be lived in experience; such is the importance of Thales's demonstration in the sands of Egypt. We can perform the same act and consider its meaning in our lives. The continually evolving knowledge of science now requires a parallel activity in the production of myths that translate and accommodate such transformations within the fabric of human affairs, permitting us to engage emotionally and physically the increasing changes in our lives.

Serres's cautionary tale demonstrates that all such transformations of knowledge involve a loss whose circumstances are remembered in a sacrificial myth. What form will this myth take in architecture? This is significant since architecture continues to ally itself with the positivist notion of a future uncritically tied to progress in technology. But we find that technology produces as many problems as it solves; a future that "advances" the human condition is questionable, but technology remains a necessary aspect of modern life. Rather than advancing toward a better future or retreating toward an irretrievable past, we find ourselves moving forward while remaining in the same place, caught in a "profound immobility where progress becomes routine."[7] The retrieval and exercise of knowledge becomes a critical counteractivity in this regard, one that architecture must engage if it is to avoid the mesmerizing attractions of science and its claims of progress.

Since 1986 the Architecture Studio at Cranbrook has addressed these concerns in a number of ways. We realized that despite long traditions of geometric and spatial references in architecture, temporal concerns are still present in the building processes upon which architecture depends.

We found that rather than eliminating time from construction, the use of geometry allied building processes with the "dark" knowledge of the body. Despite the increasing rationalization of

I-96 (Jefferies Freeway) north of Grand Boulevard, Detroit, Michigan, 1987–1988 by Douglas Aikenhead

construction processes through the use of industrialized methods and products, building remains a labor-intensive activity largely informed by the circumstances surrounding the involuntary actions of the body. But these temporal concerns are no longer the direct charge of architects, whose role is now limited to the representational and legal description of the building on its site. Architects have thus become increasingly preoccupied with describing a proposed building as an abstraction rather than as a collection of processes that occur over time.

The Architecture Studio, located between Detroit and its expanding suburbs, has also noticed that architecture, despite its symbolic value as an enduring presence, now appears and disappears with the frequency of consumer objects. Traveling around the region, one is always between the activities of building and unbuilding, between the rapid suburban development that transforms vast tracts of land into construction sites and the equally rapid abandonment and razing found in large parts of the city. We have also noted how shifting real-estate values shorten the life span of commercial structures in the region's middle zone, causing them to be torn down or renovated as frequently as once a decade. Buildings do not last as long as they once did, and architecture can no longer claim to symbolize stable and enduring culture.

Robert Smithson noted this phenomena in his seminal essay "A Tour of the Monuments of Passaic New Jersey."[8] Smithson argues that the "monuments" of Passaic, a former industrial town, are not to be found on pedestals but instead in the abandoned industrial structures and new infrastructure projects such as highways and sewer lines. While the old industrial buildings with their crumbling walls and rusted beams could justifiably be considered ruins in the romantic sense, Smithson notes that the new construction projects are also in a perpetual state of disorder. He terms such constructions "ruins in reverse" and describes the activity on their sites as "building into ruin." For Smithson, the building environment is evidence of a process of disorder rather than of order and is better described by the law of entropy than by the spatial and symbolic forms of geometry. Though one could argue that new constructions bring matter to a higher level of order, what interests me is how Smithson sees the environment charged by the force or effect of time rather than of space, recognizing that the stuff of building is always in a state of movement or transition from one state to another.

Thus one becomes aware of a building's mortality, that a building and our own bodies have something in common. The ideal building exists only at the brief moment when the last brick is laid, then begins the long and sometimes wonderful history of its decline. This has inspired the Studio to study architecture in ways overlooked in contemporary architectural practice, seeking to interpret the stuff of Serres's third shadow, the dark knowledge of the temporal body gained through experience and refined through repetitive tasks and empirical investigation.

One key to this knowledge lies in the verbs we use to describe the processes engaged in transforming material: to fold, to cut, to bind, to split. The list forms an encyclopedia of process whose extent testifies to the knowledge of physical and bodily acts available to us.[9] It is also remarkable that such actions have been with us from the beginning of history, enabling and defining our embodied relationship to material. The work that follows can be understood as a research into the possibilities residing in such verbs.

Perhaps the most direct examples of this practice in the Studio's work are the exercises given in the first months of the program. These are typically delivered in short statements that demonstrate the potential of a verb. For example, in the problem statement "Form a Pour," forming and pouring are tied together as related activities. The architectural implications of such actions are obvious to the extent that forming and pouring concrete are frequently performed on construction sites. Significant in this case is that the problem has been given to architects rather than contractors or "builders," asking them to consider the form of a pour as a direct outcome of the process by which it is made while weighing its *architectural* implications.

Form a Pour by Brent Kovalchick

The problem statements also force one to reconsider how language is used to define a building process. The problem "Make a Temporal Section" implies that time can be rendered within a conventional form of architectural representation. Adam Womelsdorf's solution uses fire as the temporal principle. He stacked layers of gridded wood and lit a fire within the volume. The unstacking of the burnt-out layers revealed the sectional aspects of the flame.

As can be seen, the body is closely involved in the production of such work. Its limits are explored more directly in the problem "Body Measure, Measured Body" where the fixed, spatial aspect of measurement is set against the variable and complex qualities of the body itself, with the implication that these conditions might also be used to form the basis of a measure. This latter possibility is explored by Jeanine Centuori with a device that translates unconscious movements of the body into the two dimensional form of a drawing. The accompanying photograph shows the device mounted above the

Make a Temporal Section by Adam Womelsdorf

head of the subject with a string connecting her hand to a pencil which is activated by the movements of the body. The resulting drawings not only enable us to measure the extent of

Make a Temporal Section by Adam Womelsdorf

such movements but also give us a picture of that which we normally cannot see: a body measure that acts as an index of our own movements in the world.

Such process-oriented work is best documented using recording rather than representational methods. This distinction is critical to the Studio's work in that it calls attention to the limitations of conventional architectural representation in conveying a temporal dimension. As Serres indicates, the geometry upon which the conventions of plan, section, and elevation are based posits a stable reference point in space. Architectural representation is keyed to this reference and develops its assumptions accordingly. A recording, on the other hand, conveys a phenomena over time. One definition describes recording as the transference of a phenomenon from one surface to another: a tape recorder inscribes sound onto tape and plays it back so that it can be received upon the surface of the ear. Photography can be considered as an optical recording device, conveying light through its chemical impression on a light-sensitive surface. Though a singular impression, the photograph signifies one moment out of the continuum of time, a puncture in the temporal envelope. The photograph nonetheless remains subjective. The single photograph is always *selected* from a field of view, a temporal and spatial context inferred by its singular perspective. Taking a picture is an act of interpretation. The Studio attempts to achieve just this sense of an encompassing moment in the act of *recording* its work. Architecture occurs within a field of encompassing, environmental concerns not adequately conveyed and analyzed via conventional means of representation.

As a result, the studio building itself has become an unwitting participant in the work; its walls, floor, and ceilings appear as a backdrop to the various constructions. These not only act within the space but *activate* it through their performative aspects. Architecture is thus enriched through its ability to inspire and organize actions, each leaving a trace or memory upon its surface. The record of the Studio is imbedded within the dark spaces of the building (like the cave, it has no windows), its lessons emerging from the temporal shadows in the form of photo-synthetic documents.

The height of the pyramid is not the only knowledge contained in the darkness of the third shadow. Upon entering, we have found its interior replete with the actions and efforts of builders who have come before. For Thales, the illumination of the shadow provided a view into the Aleph, making all things transparent to thought. It is possible that we are just now waking up from his dream.

Body Measure: Device
by Jeanine Centuori

Body Measure: Drawing
by Jeanine Centuori

Notes

1. Michel Serres, *Hermes: Literature, Science, Philosophy* (Baltimore: Johns Hopkins University Press, 1982), 84.

2. Serres, *Hermes*, 86.

3. Aristotle's *Physics,* as quoted in Richard Sorabji, *Matter, Space and Motion* (Ithaca, N.Y.: Cornell University Press, 1988), 186.

4. Joseph J. Kockelmans and Theodore J. Kisiel, *Phenomenology and the Natural Sciences* (Evanston, Ill.: Northwestern University Press, 1970), 54.

5. Henri Bergson, *Matter and Memory* (New York: Zone Books, 1991), 186.

6. Denis Hollier, *Against Architecture* (Cambridge: MIT Press, 1989), 57.

7. Gianni Vattimo, *The End of Modernity* (Baltimore: Johns Hopkins University Press, 1988), 7.

8. Robert Smithson, *The Writings of Robert Smithson* (New York: New York University Press, 1979), 54.

9. For an exhaustive list of process verbs see Richard Serra, "Verb List, 1967–68," first published in Gregoire Muller, *The New Avant-Garde: Issues for the Art of the Seventies* (New York: Praeger, 1972).

Architecture Studio

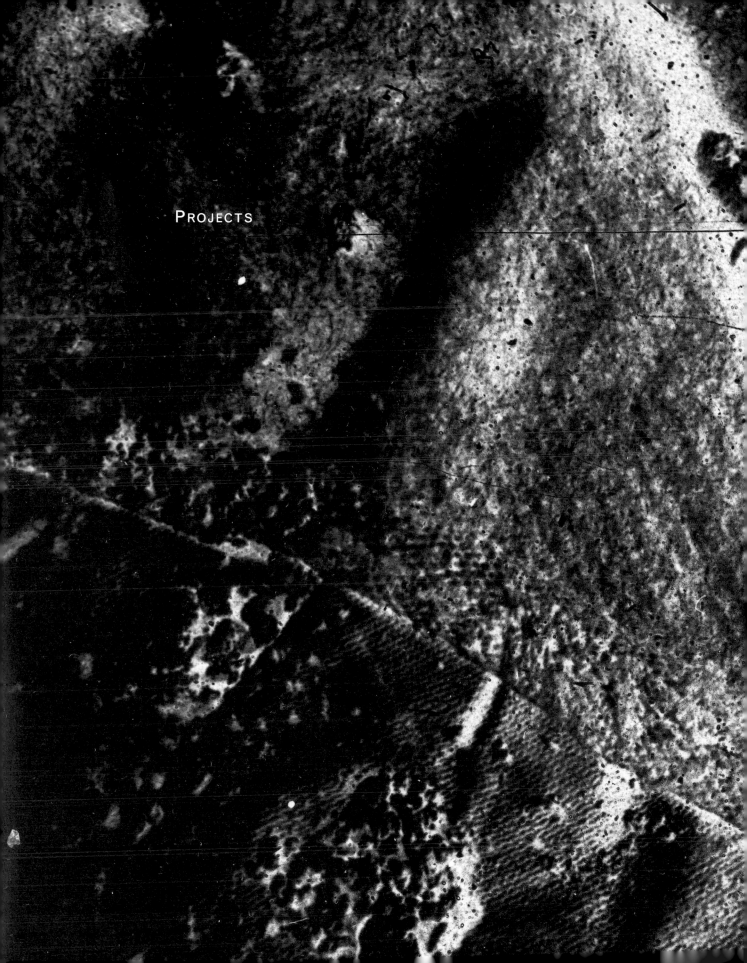

PROJECTS

Labyrinth
March–May 1988

Work by Terence Van Elslander

In "The Thing," Heidegger writes of our modern relationship to the things of the world. He notes that despite advances in travel and communication and the apparent reduction of the distance between one place and another, we do not find ourselves correspondingly closer to things.

"What is happening here when, as a result of the abolition of great distances, everything is equally far and equally near? What is this uniformity in which everything is neither far nor near—is, as it were, without distance?"[1]

Heidegger then argues that the problem of distance comes not from the idea of physical proximity but from the manner with which we construct our relationship to the things of the world. Things remain apart from us because we have chosen to include an abstract point of view in the embodied perception of what appears before us. Seeing something in this manner assumes that it is present as both a perception and an idea, placing it in a relativistic balance between that which is tangible and that which is abstract. To locate a thing in space means to perceive it visually as well as to locate it within the context of an abstract framework. In such a way the place that a thing inhabits is separated from the existential weight (or distance) that it may offer.

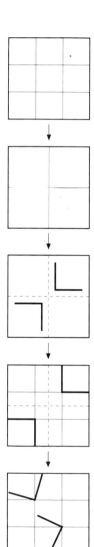

By structuring itself according to distanceless abstractions as represented by the conventions of plan and elevation, modern architecture participates in the dislocation between inhabitation and location. Something is always left out in the experience of a modern building because the ideal references of the plan or elevation can never be simultaneous with our sense of inhabitation. The space between these two conditions of seeing is an impossible one, a labyrinth out of which we can never find our way. This is the space that modern architecture asks us to inhabit. It is a trap that we can leave only by splitting the mind from the body.

Van Elslander's labyrinth is constructed on a nine-square grid of steel panels. The nine squares are emblematic of the primary condition of bodily enclosure because they are the fewest needed to define a planimetric interior. Set against the nine squares are two L-shaped panels on pivot hinges positioned on diagonally opposite corners of the central square. The sides of these panels may derive either from the enclosure of the primary, interior square or from a displaced four-square intersection, the primary sign of location, or quincunx, in Cartesian geometry. Its instability arises from the opposition of bodily enclosure and conceptual location implied by these two forms.

For Van Elslander, the labyrinth is a trap in which one is caught between the lived space of the body and the conceptual space of the mind, an endless threshold reconfigured with every passage. The motion of rotational enfolding continues within the thickness of the plaster panels set into the steel-framed walls. These are constructed via a process that repeatedly forms, breaks, and recasts each panel, enfolding the surface of the original into the interior of its section. A labyrinth of infinite folds and turns results, making a structure of in-between that is the intersection of transcendent and embodied vision.

Notes

1. Martin Heidegger, "The Thing," in *Poetry, Language, Thought* (New York: Harper and Row, 1975), 166.

Dreams of Opacity

October 1986–April 1987

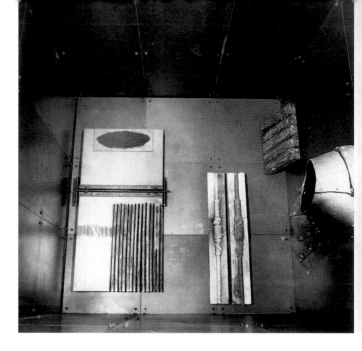

Box of Steel

Work by Frank Fantauzzi

In 1983 the sculptor Joseph Beuys lined the entire Konrad Fischer Gallery (ceiling, floor, and walls) with copper sheeting. He also removed the door of the gallery, which was located on a narrow street in the medieval section of Düsseldorf, thereby permitting anyone to enter. The installation, entitled *Lung,* opened a breathing space in a tight section of the city. The thought of being surrounded by copper evokes a flood of associations, as if the metal possesses a repository of images that enters the body through all of its pores. The immediate associations are evident: copper is commonly used to convey, store, and shed liquids. Copper pipes, roofs, and pots come to mind along with their textures, colors, and smells. Beuys created an intermediate space between a roof and a pot, an interior and an exterior. Here the fluids of the city mingled, the tangy acids transforming the copper from dark brown to green.

Why has contemporary architecture forsaken such a rich ground of associations, the dreams imbedded in the darkness of material?

Frank Fantauzzi's work also dwells upon the poetic associations found in material. "Dreams of Opacity" affords a glimpse beyond the surface, into the embodied spaces that materials can provoke.

24

Box of Lead

Box of Stool Metals are the foundation of earth, its deepest elements. They arise from the depths, from the heat. They also reside in the cosmos, in the heat of stars. In between are tools fashioned by steel, tools that cut through the flesh of time.

Box of Lead Lead is the anchor, the base, of metals. Lead deadens, drawing energy into itself and neutralizing it, folding over upon itself to bury all traces within its opacity, always seeking to return to its own interior. The slowness and malleability of lead are insidious. Readily inhabiting its form, lead kills its host object through suffocation. The box of lead is a tomb. Nothing escapes here; all sound is deadened, all light is smothered.

Architecture Studio

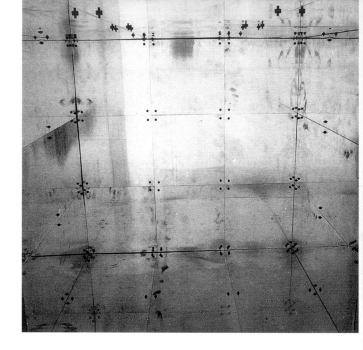

Box of Copper

Four crates sit in a gallery. From a distance, the boxes appear closed and complement the room's empty white walls. Both surfaces await transformation, the boxes by their as yet invisible interiors and the walls by works yet to be hung. Approaching the boxes, one notices that their tops are open and that each is lined with a different material: lead, steel, copper, glass. The overt material quality of these interiors comes as a surprise, affording glimpses of four different worlds within the "neutral" space of the museum. Gazing into each box, we see an assortment of objects inspired by the nature and processes of its respective material. In the case of lead, for example, the box contains a number of wrappings, demonstrating lead's malleability and its ability to assume any form. At the bottom of the box lies a lead sheet folded like cloth alongside a number of mysterious objects. We are drawn into the deadening quiet of the interior where, as in Beuys's *Lung,* the dreams and associations locked within the material are released.

Box of Glass

Box of Copper Copper is the color of warmth, a glow in the darkness of earth. Copper is found in veins, traces of eruptions from the depths, from the primary fire, preserved in its brightness. The heat still flows in its veins as electricity. In contact with the atmosphere copper exfoliates into green, shedding water like the leaves of a plant. It keeps moving.

Box of Glass Glass is the material of vision. It creates the transparency of the lens and offers an invisible door to the soul. Glass enables us to see farther and deeper. It makes the world transparent and poses the dilemma of boundaries.

Photography was born on glass, which has become the surface of our representations. We are surrounded by the images that it reflects back on us. How can we escape this circle? How can we find an opacity through which to crawl?

Erasing Detroit

September–October 1991

Work by Dan Hoffman

One of the major issues in a recent mayoral race in Detroit was the amount of public money to be spent on removing abandoned structures in the city. They were seen as a danger to the surrounding neighborhoods because they were often set on fire or used for drug deals. The selective removal of housing stock has become a standard procedure in this beleaguered city. Little or no housing is being built to replace that which has been removed. Unbuilding has surpassed building as the city's major architectural activity.

This work attempts to come to grips with this development. The sites of removed dwellings are covered with black paint on aerial photographs of the city. This procedure parallels that of the city government charts, which indicate open land parcels by blacking them out. The resulting patterns indicate that unbuilding overwhelms building and makes us consider erasure as a significant force in the urban environment.

I hope that by rendering this erasure at a comprehensive scale another "view" of the city and culture will emerge, a view free of the positivist prejudice that still determines much of our architectural vision.

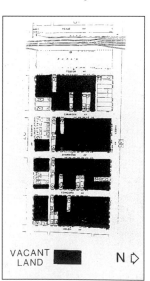

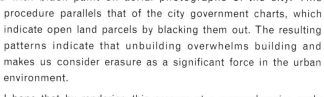

Vacant Land Map issued by the
city of Detroit

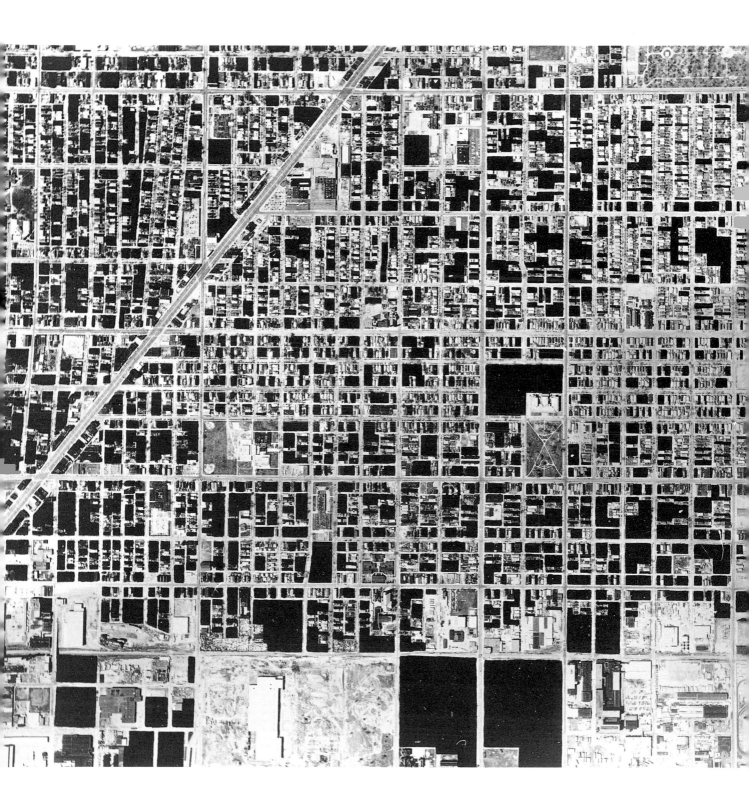

29

The building of the Tower of Babel represents humankind's attempt to reach the infinite point of view of God, the place from which all constructions are seen in their ideal way: as plans. The destruction of the tower has been read as a metaphor for the plan's necessary invisibility, for as much as we desire to act according to its rules we remain oblivious to its effects.

9119 St. Cyril

January 1988

Work by Jean-Claude Azar, James Cathcart, Frank Fantauzzi, Terence Van Elslander, and Michael Williams

As shown in the previous work, "Erasing Detroit," large portions of Detroit are being transformed through the abandonment and subsequent demolition of houses and neighborhoods. This phenomenon has profoundly affected members of the Architecture Studio, opening our eyes to the phenomena of unbuilding, often overlooked in contemporary discussions on architecture. We chose the term *unbuilding* over *destruction* and *deconstruction* because the processes involved are neither anarchic nor critical. The removal of built structures has become a significant industry in the city, with demolition contractors bidding to clear large lots. The industries that once employed workers and the economies that support the development of cities no longer view the city as having a value beyond providing services to consume their latest products. The city is expendable in their eyes; their global economic interests make local concerns such as the architecture and qualities of a place minor considerations.

The choice to work within this context of unbuilding is a difficult one, since much of the ideology of architecture supports the organization of materials and energies toward the positivist idea of a building as a perfected instrument, however temporary it may be. The reversal, or unmaking, of the assumptions of architectural practice is a significant aspect of this project and was manifested in many ways, from the detailed consideration of methods to take down the house (purchased from a demolition contractor for one dollar) to the way in which the architects involved themselves directly in the physical aspects of the work. The project even reversed the accepted architectural practice of beginning with a two-dimensional representation, such as a plan, and expanding it into the volume of a building. By starting with a building rather than a representation, the architects *discovered* the plan through a process of excavation. The plan, therefore, resulted from the weighing and sorting of what it once supported, as discussed in the architects' account of the process:

"The house transformed itself into successive states. . . . At one point the house was entirely plaster, at another, all wood. Our labor was confined to splitting the house, loosening its fastenings, and overcoming the forces of friction which kept the house in an unrequited relationship with the forces of gravity."

The project is documented in a series of "construction photographs" showing successive states of unbuilding. These are more than simple documentation. They offer a privileged view of a process that has become part of the background activity of the city, a silent lament that recalls the ritual slow-motion torture of children that ends Passolini's film *Salo.* By extending this process in time (the house could have been demolished in less than a day using heavy machinery), the architects delayed the inevitable, producing an opening through which we gain a brief critical distance from the dominant view of architecture and building that blinds us to the erasure of our environment.

The poignancy of this act of unmaking is brought home, as it were, in the gallery, where the house remained for a time condensed into piles of material. In a corner, away from the piles, sat a small metal box filled with photographs and letters found in the walls during the unmaking of the house.

The piles of material were weighed against the body of memories that once made the house a home. The erasure of the evidence of this memory is the subject of this work.

Memory-Place
October 1988–April 1989

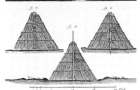

"Rural Economy: Wood Carbon"
from Diderot's *Encyclopedia*

Work by Richard Parrish

Studio members often turn to Diderot's *Encyclopedia*[1] for information on preindustrial means of fabrication. Though the encyclopedia intended to rationalize eighteenth-century material arts and render them as forms of production, the book possesses a mysterious quality that no amount of analysis can abstract. This is most evident in explanations of processes that evolved outside the Enlightenment's rational and geometric forms of knowledge, cases such as hunting birds and tying knots. These premodern forms of knowledge depended on the body's ability to develop and remember certain actions. Indeed, the *Encyclopedia* signals the beginning of the decline of such knowledge, shifting from a direct transmission within guild and family structures to the more general and abstract book form. Modern writers such as Proust understood that our ability to recall the past is intimately tied to the actions of our bodies and to the sensual qualities of materials. Thus arises the question of whether specific memories can be retrieved through reenacting bodily acts.

Richard Parrish's desire to recover aspects of his past led him to reengage the actions and materials of a childhood spent on the North American prairie. He hoped that this activity would recall the place of his early encounters with building.

Parrish began his work with a construction recalling the wooden fences that bounded the prairie. Their straight posts and slats also evoked the regular rows of planting and the other forms that are the signs of human dwelling. Next he drew earth up around the construction, forming a primitive hut that was then transformed by burning out its interior. This significant act embodied the symbolism of the hearth and also marked the memory of the construction with a cataclysmic event. (Similarly a "thermal sympathy"[2] was effected by making a construction of and for the body.) By breaking open the dwelling/vessel, Parrish released its memories to find new places and constructions.

Notes

1. Denis Diderot, *Encyclopédie, ou Dictionnaire des sciences, des arts et des métiers* (1751–76; reprint, New York: Harry N. Abrams, Inc., 1978).

2. Gaston Bachelard, *The Psychoanalysis of Fire* (Boston: Beacon Press, 1964), 40.

Wall-Sieve

Work by Julieanna Preston

The architect Raimund Abraham once noted, with some envy one supposes, that architects in Palladio's time did not have to make detailed drawings of the contents of a wall section. Abraham speculated that the contents of the section were common knowledge among masons and that the architect's role was directed toward delineating its form and extent. One could add that the masonry walls of the time were all made of gradations of the same material, from the large rubble stones in the interior to the finely ground pigments of the finished plaster coat. This material continuity rendered the uniform poché of an architectural section an accurate diagram of its physical properties, focusing the eye on the manner in which light articulates the spatial volumes on either side of the wall.

Contemporary wall sections are another matter, informed more by evolving technology and production than by local building traditions and their formal poetics. The section through the exterior wall of a typical suburban house consists of at least eight distinct layers, each designed for a different function, ranging from the control of temperature, humidity, and sunlight to the building's support. Such functions proliferate as technology refines what private and public bodies require to exist in the contemporary environment.

The wall section today is more an active skin than an abstract thickness defining a relationship between interior and exterior. Each layer of this skin filters a bodily concern through a layer of technological production to the point that, along with Merleau-Ponty, we might say that the world is made of the same stuff as the body.[1]

Julieanna Preston's "Wall-Sieve" meditated on the contemporary wall section. Layers of copper, straw, cloth and sawdust, and oilcloth filtered particular bodily fluids or qualities. The layers hung on the interior walls of a wooden crate covered on the exterior with a layer of drywall painted the color of the room in which the construction was installed. This final layer would appear to be a concession to the idea of the wall as the distinct limit between interior and exterior, but the partially opened box and the photographic sections shown nearby demonstrate that this layer is the thinnest of all. Preston applied it more as a contextual adaptation to the gallery environment than as a sign of the indeterminate thickness of a Palladian section.

Continuing the comparison, it is difficult to imagine the wall-sieve rendered with the precision of a drypoint stylus. Drawings of the wall-sieve would exist in a more fluid and permeable environment. Marks on the page would record rather than represent, acting as stains rather than as abstract symbols. Preston's drawings explore this permeable space where interior and exterior seep into each other at different rates of flow, rendering the color black more as substance than as void. As Studio member Iwonka Piotrowska has put it, "Matter is trapped movement."[2] For Preston, space is a medium of bodily flows; the wall is a sieve into a room. There are no edges in this architecture, just extended thresholds between one bodily condition and the next.

Notes

1. Maurice Merleau-Ponty, *The Primacy of Perception* (Evanston, Ill.: Northwestern University Press, 1964), 164.

2. Iwonka Piotrowska. "Finding Ground" (Master's thesis, Cranbrook Academy of Art, 1993).

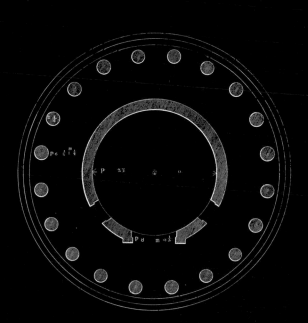

Plan of the Temple of Vesta by Andrea Palladio

Centering Device
September 1989–April 1990

Work by Brent Kovalchik

The *Vitruvian Man* by Leonardo da Vinci is often cited as an example of the intersection of the Neoplatonic belief in the existence of pure geometric forms and the belief in humans as the symbol of God on earth. The primary geometric forms of circle and square are clearly indicated, with the figure's extended limbs drawn precisely on them. Here geometry and body coincide. The question always asked is, Which form produces the other? Is geometry a product of the body or is geometry a form to which the body aspires?

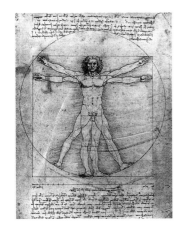

Da Vinci's other figure studies fail to answer. Rather than using geometry as a symbolic form to frame the body, da Vinci employs it to determine the form of the body's potential for movement. Centers and radii locate points of rotation and the direction of trajectories. Geometry here is an analytical tool that translates into mechanisms that can reproduce the dynamic actions of the body in nature, so that the body can connect to the turbulent energies of the cosmos.

Vitruvian Man by Leonardo da Vinci (Accademia, Venice, Italy. Photograph by Alinari/Art Resource, New York)

In the da Vinci diagram each limb is located in relation to its point of rotation. For example, the center lines of the legs extend to intersect in the navel, even though their joints are in the hips. This extended "center of rotation" enables da Vinci to consider the body as a machine that produces a force that can be extended by mechanisms such as geared or rotational levers. The force can then be applied to achieve specific effects. Examples of mechanisms that allow individuals to propel themselves through the air, land, and water appear throughout da Vinci's notebooks. Humans are divine because they participate in the *movement* of nature. Geometry is the tool, and mechanisms are the vehicle.

Is it possible to reconsider how the body and its latent force were used in Renaissance architecture? This question forms the basis of Kovalchik's project. Preparatory sketches propose a device to position the body so that it can act as a precise vertical axis around which to construct an enclosure of brick according to the rotational profile of its outstretched limbs. The resulting enclosure is similar in form to that of da Vinci's extended man rotated around the vertical axis.

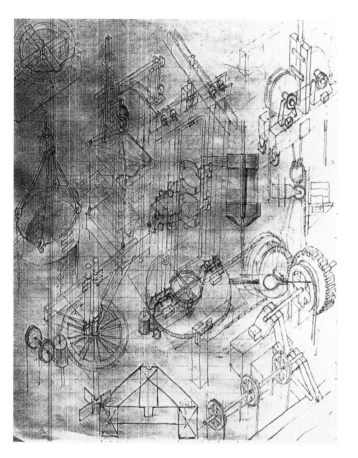 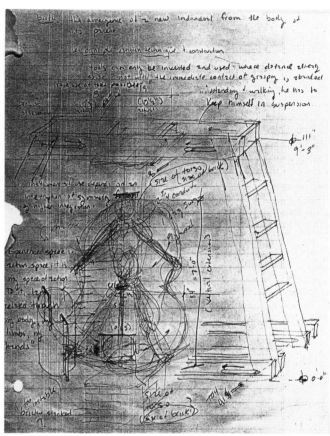

The critical aspect of the project is the demonstration of how the economy and function of such a mechanism depend on a strict and symmetrical adherence to the axis of movement. All activities must be organized according to a single principle, from mixing the mortar to loading and unloading the bricks. The mechanism turns entirely by the effort of one body and is limited to the stationary axis of motion.

Da Vinci's mechanisms do not possess the autonomous movement of modern machines since their actions are tied to the movement of the body that propels them. Modern autonomy was made possible when the relationship between geometry and the body was severed, resulting in motions that can accelerate beyond comprehension. Today we look back on da Vinci's mechanisms as a respite from the delirium of motion, and we are comforted by the illusion of occupying the center now that life is lived at the edge.

Divisible by Two (House of Snouts)

February–April 1990

The more abstract the truth is that you would teach, the more you have to seduce the senses to it.

—Nietzsche, *Beyond Good and Evil*

Work by Jean-Claude Azar

Gilles Deleuze describes a baroque house consisting of two parts: the upper part is a single, enclosed chamber with no windows; below is a horizontally extended suite of rooms with windows that admit the knowledge available to the senses. Between the two are "folds in matter,"[1] internal structures that connect the material and perceptual qualities admitted into the first floor with the conceptual abstractions of the second. The lower floor extends on all sides, incorporating myriad aspects of experience, while the upper floor remains closed, its walls lined with the folds and pleats of matter connected through the roof with the infinite, which organizes the bundle in chordal harmonies.

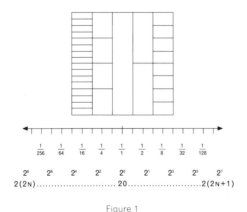

Figure 1

This binary structure is not fixed in a discrete space. The folds in matter are temporal. Matter flows through them as water flows through a wave caught in the current. Folds are attractors that organize the flow, channeling movement into bundles of folds that extend to the infinite.

The House of Snouts is a model of the baroque structure of knowledge as described by Deleuze, a model built on the numerical extrapolations of a fold that is folded upon itself: a double fold that expands according to a series that itself is driven by the factor of two. The model is also divided into two parts, the upper consisting of a steel cube open at the top and the lower of a set of chambers lined by a double thickness of rubber sheeting which expands when the upper chamber is filled with plaster.

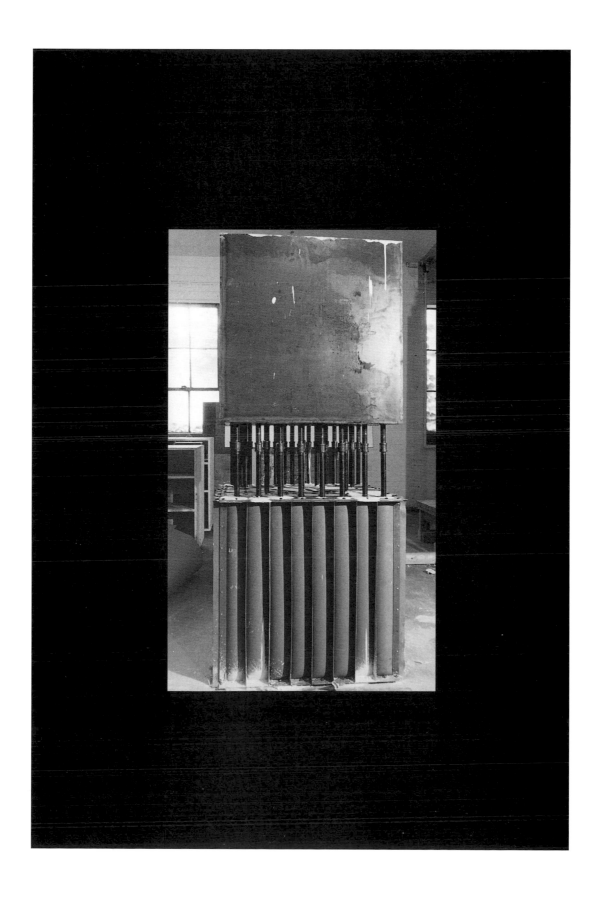

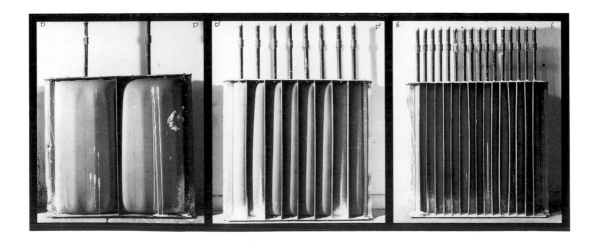

The plan of the lower section is divided into chambers divided by the opposing exponential series $2(2n)$ and $2(2n+1)$ that diverge to the left and right of the central chamber (figure 1). Connecting the chambers in a continuous series of folds is the double-layered rubber bladder (figure 2) which, when extended, forms the continuous series of divisions by two (figure 3).[2]

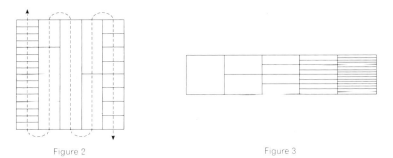

Figure 2   Figure 3

Like the baroque house, the House of Snouts is imbued with the dynamic energies of the fold. Plaster, the material of the baroque, charges the system. Plaster's fine grain enables it to be formed into wild and turbulent flows that express the dynamic interaction between force and matter. In Azar's model, however, these energies channel into the fecund power of the numerical sequence that brackets the folded rubber sheets. These are filled when the upper cube is charged with plaster, which empties into the numerical chambers through the conveying snouts. The one is divided into the many, which proliferate into an infinity of chambers.

When filled, the double layer of rubber sheeting expands toward the rectangular perimeters of the individual chambers, forming "bladders" that press against each other, recalling the perceptual aspects of the lower floor of the baroque house. The continuity of the folded sheet stretches to its limit; a linear equation transforms into an exponential curve that approaches the surface area of the chamber. With each division of the chamber the ratio of linear sheet to surface area increases to the point where, theoretically, the two are equal. When the skin equals the volume that it contains, when the plaster is folded into the rubber, the point of infinity has been reached. In these extremes the union of substance and structure, matter and mind, occurs, vibrating through the fold to infuse us with the sensuous play of limits.

Notes

1. Gilles Deleuze, *The Fold: Leibniz and the Baroque* (Minneapolis: University of Minnesota Press, 1993), 3.

2. Mark Bartlett, in an article entitled "An Avatar of the Tortoise" (*Work + Text* [Bloomfield Hills: Cranbrook Academy of Art, 1991]), argues that the difference in these two numerical series is the core of Azar's work, pointing out that when opposed in such a manner (figure 1), the two series act as the inverse of the periodicity of a pendulum, growing rather than diminishing in number. Bartlett also reminds us that Zeno's paradox functions on the principle that space is infinitely divisible and therefore is always divisible by two.

Necessary Frictions

January–May 1990

Work by Michael Williams

Because the body is opaque to itself, consciousness seeks to find its place amid the objects of the world. Every object presents itself as a particular configuration of resistance to the body. By engaging the object, the body comes to know itself, each object inscribing a particular trace upon the embodied map of consciousness. This referential knowledge of the body can never be complete, for the body (and other bodies) exists through the transformations of time. The opacity follows us like a shadow, passing behind the objects of the world and rendering them in relief as things apart from us.

Gaston Bachelard uses the phrase *coefficient of adversity* to define more precisely this relationship between the body and the objects of the world. A coefficient denotes a given factor (itself a relationship) used to reference an equation between two different aspects of a phenomenon. A coefficient is a constant of variability that gives proportion to the different parts of an equation. The term *adversity* captures the actively mutable relationship between the body and its objects, acknowledging that an object's resistance is felt during an intentional bodily act. Adversity projects its presence, and resistance gathers its latent forces. For example, a door presents itself in terms of the adversity projected in opening it. The details of the door (its hinges, handle, and construction) anticipate the exertion of the body upon it in the act of opening. A chair, on the other hand, does not project adversity but anticipates release from adversity, signaling potential relief from the burden of upright posture.

Williams suspends the typical use of the chair as an instrument for sitting, treating the chair as an object of inspection rather than use. The chair becomes a site for investigation, its various surfaces offering themselves for inspection and intervention.

The investigation of the act of grasping the chair's seat anticipates the position and form of hands by securing felt pads to the chair with steel brackets. The intervention also records the interaction between hand and chair, providing a middle zone between subject and object, between the surface of the body and the surface of the chair.

Felt absorbs the compression of the grasp and the load of the movement of the chair. Rubber and steel wire create a tensile load within the chair-site. The specific tension on the rubber adjusts to the specific load of the chair when lifted from the indicated position. These devices are signs of the chair's possible interaction with the body, part of the projection of adversity.

The catalog of relationships between the body and the object is open-ended. Each contact demands a different recording instrument. For example, the horizontal movement of the chair along a surface is to be recorded. The contact between hand

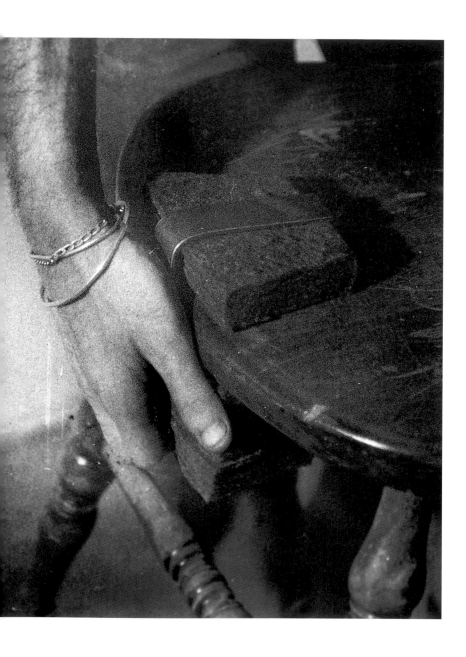

and chair is not directly addressed; rather, the chair is implicated in the instrumentality of its own recording. A pointed lead weight is affixed to the bottom of the chair to trace the movement of the pull via the chair and the surface along which it is pulled. The lead weight also serves as a counterweight to the movement of the chair's rotation around its back legs.

The surface upon which the movement is recorded is a layer of grease spread on a steel sheet. The choice of the grease as a recording surface reveals a precise understanding of the poetic function latent in

recording. Grease is often used to reduce friction between two surfaces. It is also a sign for the inevitable frictions of recording, which involves a transfer.

A recording is a transfer from one surface to another over time. Measurement, on the other hand, occurs in time but always with reference to a specific point outside time. This point is the end according to which the means of measure are organized. The ends of a recording are not fixed. Its point, if this metaphor holds, is to reproduce the phenomenon exactly.

Williams's preoccupation with the surface of recordings reflects a parallel fascination with vision and the mechanisms of inspection. Sight and touch relate through the instrument of the body. Sight is the anticipation of touch; its projection makes way for the receptive faculties in the hand and fingers. Williams's obsessive documentation of his work intends to bring these two aspects of perception together outside the body.

The camera itself is an indexical recording device wherein light reflected off the surface of objects

transfers directly to the surface of the photographic film via the perspective of the lens. The instant of the photograph is the temporal "point" of vision, separating time into a before and an after. When we examine a photograph we understand that time has taken place, that light has warmed the surface of the film over the brief instant that the shutter was open. The perspectival hole in the visual field made possible by the lens enables the delivery of light. It is as if to take a picture one must mask out all other perspectives. This singular focus isolates the horizon in a frame within which further inspection can occur.

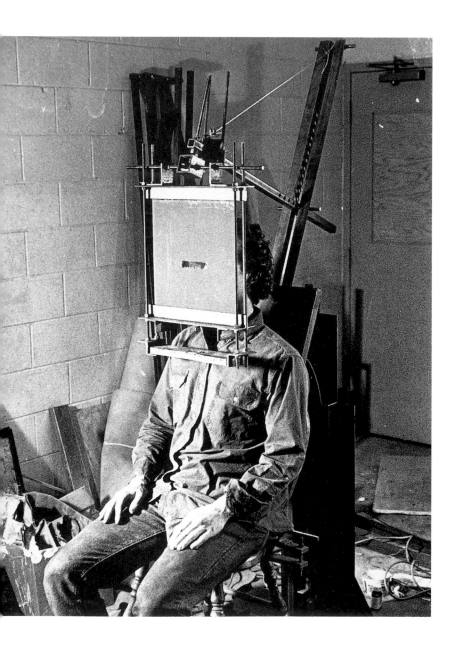

The impact of claustrophobic vision appears in a final construction in which the vision of an occupant of the chair is restricted by a steel plate with a small horizontal slot. The intricate adjustments of this focusing device recall the devices used to hold a body still over the long exposure times of the early days of photography. Here the instrumentality of the camera extends beyond the camera itself.

The work thus unfolds out of itself, one recording producing another. The chair remains roughly at the center, an unlikely object amid the dark steel devices surrounding it, precision instruments that carry a

trace of its surface into the world. The smell of the grease and felt recalls early-twentieth-century workshops, the time of great frictions. This project is an object lesson in the entropy latent in our recording endeavors. The frictions of instrumentality are not lost in the electronic field with which we have become so enamored, but have been transformed into the noise of endless interpretation. The effort of reading becomes the source of our adversity, for with each interpretation the frictions grow weaker and weaker, the contacts with the object less defined. The entropy of heat energy is paralleled by an entropy of meaning.

The Treatment of Fractures

October–November 1989

Work by Frank Fantauzzi and Michael Williams

This work involved a number of on-site architectural interventions at the Carnegie Arts Center in Covington, Kentucky. The center had just acquired a building, erected in 1902, and was considering issues of its restoration or renovation when Fantauzzi and Williams were asked to submit a project proposal. The resulting interventions were meant to provoke questions concerning the physical evidence of the structure's history and the ways in which such evidence is transformed over time through patterns of use and decay.

By entitling their work "The Treatment of Fractures," the two likened the circumstance of the old building to that of an injured body in need of repair. The analogy also implies that the repair should return the body/building to a certain idea(l) of health. The difficulty in this case was in determining what that idea(l) should be.

Jean-Paul Sartre has written that there is an aspect to our bodies that is located on the surfaces of our material surroundings:

"For human reality, to be is to-be-there; that is 'there in that chair,' 'there at that table,' 'there at the top of that mountain,' with these dimensions, this orientation, etc." [1]

We exist, then, with the conditions of the building that we inhabit. This also begins to explain why we favor the appearance of a building restored to its "original" health and suppress evidence of its inevitable decline. This state of health reflects the ideal of a timeless order, which classical architecture sought to symbolize and embody. Though we may accept death in our own bodies, we

have difficulty seeing it in the environments that we inhabit. Feeling the body in the surrounding architecture draws the architecture into the body's temporal nature and the instinctive concern with death.

The processes of decay are never as predictable and controllable as the processes of order. As a result we consider them unaesthetic and uneconomical. A building is closest to its formal, "healthy" ideal on the day of its completion; from that time on, we must deal with its decay. Fantauzzi and Williams applied various treatments with the awareness of the often-conflicting demands of order and decay on a building's physical condition. The instruments employed were not neutral in this conflict; at times they repaired and preserved the order to which the building was built and at other times hastened fracture and decay. As ambiguous as these interventions were, they reintroduced a consciousness of time passing through entropic forces in materials.

These treatments alert us to a culture that views nature as a precarious force to be balanced and stabilized. Architecture has historically symbolized this very stability, making its fracture both poignant and inevitable.

Notes

1. Jean-Paul Sartre, *Being and Nothingness* (New York: Washington Square Press, 1966), 407.

At the theater entry the viewer comes upon two slots cut out of the plaster, parallel to the slope of the floor, exposing the rough brick masonry behind. To determine whether the coursing of the bricks was level a formwork was placed against the plaster, forming a cavity within which molten lead was poured. The lead hardened, producing a line against which to measure the current level of the brick coursing.

Damaged corners and openings were treated by placing formwork over adjacent surfaces and filling it with wax.

A plumb line was placed against a newel post to reestablish its vertical position. The treads and risers of the stairway were also out of level. To establish the horizontal, a device, made from a pair of angles hinged on one side with an adjustable screw to raise or lower the angles, was placed on the stair. A ball bearing was then placed on the angles, which were adjusted until they were level.

An elliptical masonry arch spans the stairway, supporting the top landing. The arch is also covered with plaster, but it was not clear whether the arch and plaster had shifted from the geometry that ordered the original construction. To measure the possible deformation a device was inserted within the arch that retraced the arc of an ellipse with a sharp stylus against the plaster. The difference between the surface of the plaster and the depth of the inscription measured the two conditions.

7

The plaster on the stairwell walls was in the process of separating from the brick. To record and measure the process of the separation, metal knives were connected by wire to individual weights located near the stair landing. This instrumentation also quickened the inevitable separation. During a visit to the site loud crashes resounded in the space as the plaster fell on the stairway.

The main theater space is surmounted by a large dome. The emphatic centrality of
the structure begged to be tested and measured relative to the surrounding room.
To this end a line was dropped from the center of the dome and marked against the
center of the floor as determined by the surrounding walls. The photograph indicates
that the two measurements do not align. After the centering measurement the line
was tensioned to one hundred pounds, which during the length of the installation
gradually diminished to seventy pounds. The question remains as to how the thirty
pounds were absorbed into the structure.

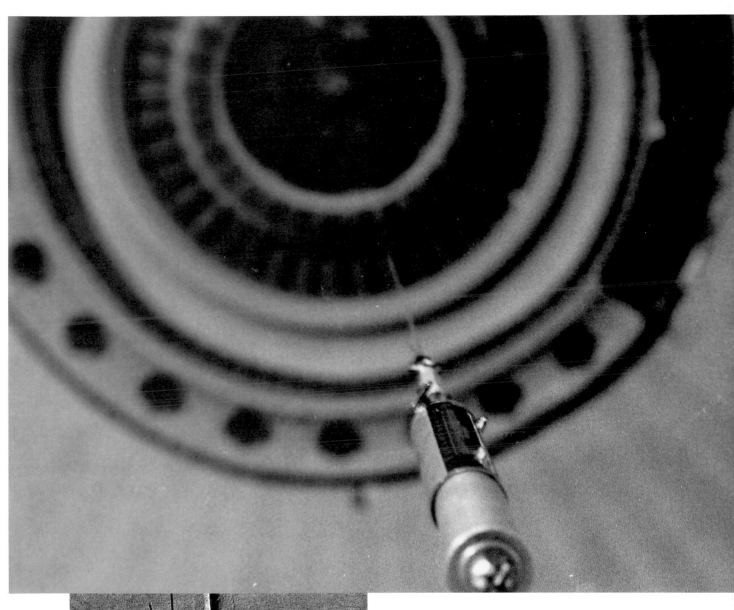

The Geometric Principle

Building in the Western tradition is an activity that has been guided by the principle of sufficient reason. This assumes that every aspect of building process can be explained through reason, an assumption that is fulfilled by structuring architecture according to geometry. This structuring forms an autonomous reference that orders building activity and makes all aspects of the process accessible to the precision of a theoretical point that exists within space and outside time.

Ordination

Ordination is the order that emerges from the stable point through rotation, division, and repetition. These activities coordinate the building according to the geometric order. Ordination establishes the authority with which to organize acts of building.

Measure

Measure extends and applies the ordination of the building. One always builds a measure upon an ordination, which is its basic reference. Measuring establishes and mediates difference.

Horizontal and Vertical

The horizontal and vertical are the primary ordinates in building. Together they constitute a crossing, an equation of balance that applies the stability of the point to the body and the world.

Instruments

Instruments serve the ordination. As the primary instruments in construction,

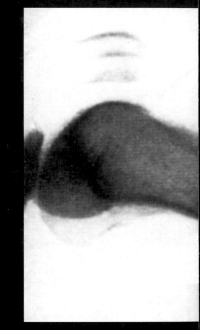

The continued refinement of instrumentation leads us to believe in the presence of the first principle in material. Refinement appears to prove reason's efficacy in the world as delivered through actions made possible by geometry. Yet the stability or certainty of geometry is attained though sacrificing time; material is transformed through time, fracturing the order of the building. Fracture here suggests a fraction of the once-complete order a measure of difference between the ordination and the real, between what exists in time and what exists out of time.

Pre-Serving Architecture

To pre-serve architecture is to maintain the ordination of a building over time. It seeks to re-member the construction, treating its fractures with instruments that recalibrate the original ordination.

Cutting In [1]

March 1990

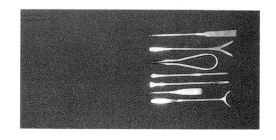

Work by David Resnick

Passages in *Moby-Dick* describe obscure nineteenth-century whaling techniques in such detail that the narrative of the great whale stops dead in its tracks, like a ship becalmed at sea. During these pauses the grain of the tale fills with the myriad details that constitute one human activity. Melville never ceases to wonder at human ingenuity, from the design of specialized tools to the systems of classification used to structure knowledge. The story's main theme is never far off, however. The precarious nature of existence, with all of its unexpected turns, lurks below the surface, rising up in a fury that strains against the patient work done in anticipation of the event. The final calamity of the story reveals its tragic dimension, demonstrating a distance between human beings and nature that can never be overcome, despite all efforts. Without this dimension the descriptions would be merely an account of the history and techniques of whaling. The description of a tool to skin a whale, for example, would be a "thing among other things" [2] rather than a symbol of the struggle to tame nature's wild heart.

The modern view is more dispassionate. There is no great struggle with nature or God outside of us, since we find ourselves implicated in the very conditions that we attempt to order and control. Nature and the "world" are no longer players on the scene against which we struggle. They are simply the disinterested background for our own actions; as Robbe-Grillet states, "Man looks at the world and the world does not look back at him." [3] A modern reading of *Moby-Dick* would therefore look to the world found in the descriptions of human activities and their tools. Here a more anthropological understanding of the text can be found, one that attempts to reconstitute a human event through the reinhabiting of its actions.

There is also more to a whale than its skin. Where, then, is this supplemental knowledge located—within the whale itself or in its relationships to its adjacent surfaces? A description brings the world to the surface of an object, creating a space for the body and a territory for possible actions. Descriptions are never neutral; they always reflect a subjective point of view. The *depth* of the described object is not within or behind it, but in the space between the body of the reader and the surface of the description, "the flesh of the world" [4] as constituted by an embodied consciousness.

The set of tools shown in this piece was made as a meditation on the lived depth of description. Inspired by a passage in *Moby-Dick* that describes the skinning of a whale, the tools are made to be reinserted into various aspects of the process. Melville writes:

> **"One of the attending harpooners now advances with a long keen weapon called a boarding-sword, and watching his chance he dexterously slices out a considerable hole in the lower part of the swaying mass. Into this hole, the end of the second alternating great tackle is then hooked so as to retain a hold upon the blubber, in order to prepare what follows. Whereupon, this accomplished swordsman, warning all hands to stand off, once more makes a scientific dash at the mass, and with a few sidelong, desperate, lunging slices, severs it completely in twain; so that while the short lower part is still fast, the long upper strip, called a blanket piece, swings clear and is ready for lowering."**[5]

Resnick is as concerned with preserving and displaying the tools as he is with their possible actions. The case constructed for this purpose has a top made of a sandwich of felt and grease that, when fastened, leaves a trace of the outlines of the individual tools. This obscure calligraphy refers us back to writing and its ability to trigger a memory of human activity. Interpreting the tools in Melville's description perpetuates this memory, enacting its schematic, written outline in renewed bodily actions.

The writing of *Moby-Dick* marked the passage of whaling from an enacted to a written form of knowledge. The great care that Melville took suggests that the descriptions are an act of mourning for a passing age, a reliving of that which has been lost. Resnick's tools demonstrate the possibilities of interpretation that exist within description. His translation from word to steel reminds us that texts exist within the web of human potential that lies in wait for the creative act.

Notes

1. From the title of chapter 67 in Herman Melville, *Moby-Dick or The Whale,* 1851.

2. Alain Robbe-Grillet, *For a New Novel: Essays on Fiction* (New York: Grove Press, 1965), 59.

3. Robbe-Grillet, *For a New Novel,* 58.

4. Maurice Merleau-Ponty, *Visible and the Invisible* (Evanston, Ill.: Northwestern University Press, 1969), 240.

5. Melville, *Moby-Dick.*

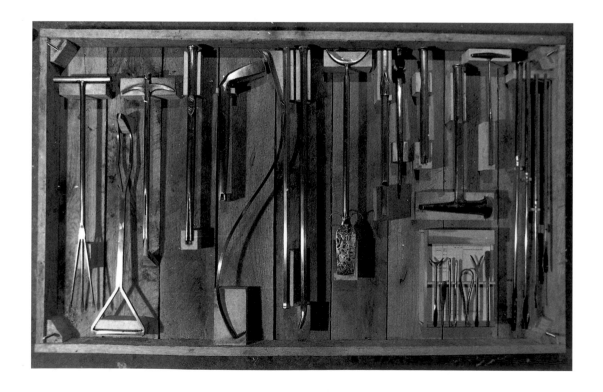

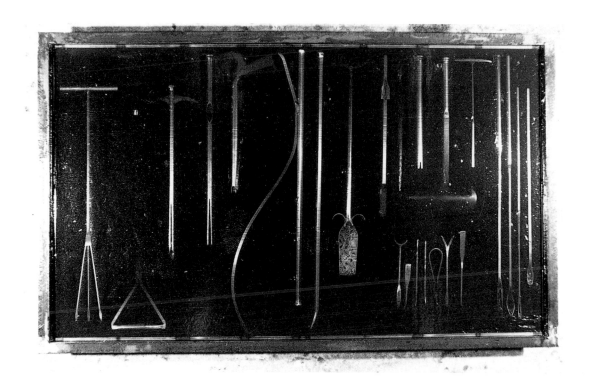

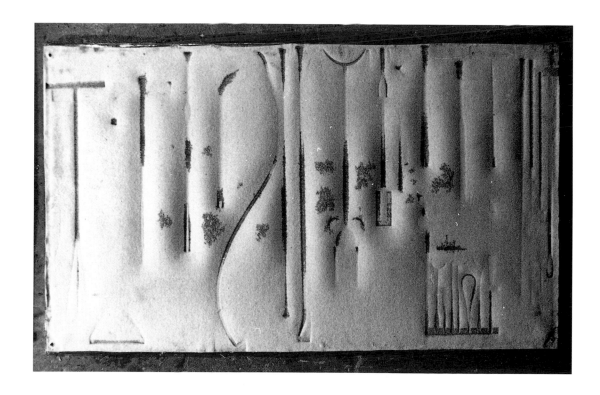

One can only read text because of the markings that are not there; the absence makes the communication possible. A blank speaks of silence: that is the other part of what a story is. While the physical material of a book has its inherent value, like the material of a body, this is not the essence. They are but containers that give presence to the story.

Blanket made from the pages
of a book

The question is, what and where is the skin of the whale?

—Herman Melville, *Moby-Dick or The Whale*

The Blanket
November 1991–May 1992

Work by Iwonka Piotrowska

After recounting the great labor of skinning the whale, Melville pauses in the chapter of *Moby-Dick* entitled "The Blanket" to reflect on the nature of the whale skin itself.[1] This mysterious and elusive subject does not lend itself to the precision of the tools described in the skinning process. One of the first difficulties that Melville encounters is visually locating where the skin begins since its outermost layer is extremely thin and transparent. Below this lies the blubber or fat, which has no distinctive surface or edge of its own but appears as "numberless obliquely crossed and re-crossed lines." The blubber is also elusive, for it has the consistency of "firm, close-grained beef, but tougher, more elastic and compact." Even the mass of the skin proves beyond our ability to comprehend fully. Melville figures that, when boiled down, it would fill more than one hundred barrels weighing ten tons—as much as the exterior walls of a good-sized wooden house.

The skin does not yield the mysteries beyond its surface. To plumb its depths we must look to either side of its indeterminate thickness. Melville responds by reflecting on the "rare virtue of a strong, individual vitality, and the rare virtue of thick walls and the rare virtue of interior spaciousness," as if the vital forces of nature also possessed an interiority beneath an insulating blanket of skin. This permits us "to live in this world without being of it" and allows the whale to travel from the polar regions to the tropics, the range of human habitation.

The gap between exterior and interior becomes a necessary space for architecture to fill. Perhaps the "spaciousness" that Melville describes is not so easily defined; as he indicates, it is not possible to locate the skin of the whale. Its interiority could be the ocean itself, a space that folds in around itself, a material with no edges—as Iwonka Piotrowska puts it, a "material where movement is held."

Piotrowska meditated on the enigma of skin through making blankets, and accompanied them with the captions shown here. Though we do not live in the ocean, Piotrowska reminds us, through Heidegger, that "on earth means under the sky." We live between the two, within the blanket that folds around us and protects us from the exterior. Architecture folds around us in the same manner. It is the fold in a space that is also a material.

Notes

1. All quotations are from chapter 68, "The Blanket," in Herman Melville, *Moby-Dick or The Whale*, 1851.

to sow
to rip up to insert to cover over again
land earth as blanket

Suspended felt blanket

Blankets are the next skin after the body. They ground us: they are our connection to earth. Being under a blanket is being in a place where I become conscious of the rest of my body as belonging to me. It is where I become conscious of the *rest* of my body as belonging to me, and everything outside of the blanket as not being of my body, and therefore, when I am under it, I am connected to the earth.

Latex blanket formed upon a brick wall

Site Extraction

February–April 1992

Work by Dean Sakamoto

Italo Calvino writes about the city of Leonia, whose residents have a passion for cleaning. Every day street cleaners remove the refuse of the city.

"Nobody wonders where, each day, they carry their load of refuse. Outside the city, surely; but each year the city expands, and the street cleaners have to fall farther back. The bulk of the outflow increases and the piles rise higher, become stratified, extend over a wider perimeter. . . . A fortress of indestructible leftovers surrounds Leonia, dominating it on every side, like a chain of mountains."[1]

This tale of refuse is familiar to inhabitants of modern cities. What was once invisible now looms before us as a fact of the urban environment, a brutal, material equation between consumption

Quarry stone extraction

and refuse that pits our environment against that which we now find necessary for our lives. This equation reminds us that our modern idea of progress is not an unhindered trajectory or an unlimited construct. Every advance or every cleaning (since an "advance" is always understood as wiping the slate clean of what existed before) produces a bit of refuse that must be accounted for, despite our desire that it disappear from view.

A corollary to the equation of consumption and refuse is what exists between building and the extraction of resources. The latter inverts the former in that the city (as a symbol of culture) grows by consuming or depleting the resources of the surrounding region. The material evidence of this function has also come to mark our environment.

Heidegger touches upon a related issue in his essay "The Question Concerning Technology," where he refers to the modern conception of nature as a "standing reserve" used for whatever purpose we require of it, be it electric power or building materials.[2] This separates us from the idea of a divine nature while still leaving us susceptible to nature's effects, since we are wholly connected to it through the medium of technology.

Dean Sakamoto became aware of this state of affairs through an early exercise in which he excavated a section of the studio's concrete floor. The manner in which he broke up and reconfigured the concrete bore a strong resemblance to the stratifications of limestone, one of cement's primary ingredients. This led Sakamoto to search for the source of limestone used in the cement in the area: a quarry in Alpena, Michigan. The immense scale of the quarry, one hundred feet high and approximately one mile in diameter, indicates the amount of material displaced from this site.

To account for this material Sakamoto began to weigh the city of Alpena against the size of the quarry and to reconsider the strata of the quarry wall in light of the initial investigations performed on the studio. Thus began a work in which the architect is, as Sakamoto states, "accountable for collecting, transporting, enframing, ordering, and preserving the limestone into an architectural condition." This profound economy of material establishes a new relationship between the architect and building that reaches beyond the confines of a structure on a site to consider our relationship to material in general.

Notes

1. Italo Calvino, *Invisible Cities* (San Diego: Harcourt Brace Jovanovich, 1974), 114–15.

2. Martin Heidegger, *The Question Concerning Technology and Other Essays* (New York: Harper Torchbooks, 1969), 16.

Studio floor extraction

Aerial photo of Alpena, Michigan, and adjacent
limestone quarry showing the displacement of quarry
stone into the city grid

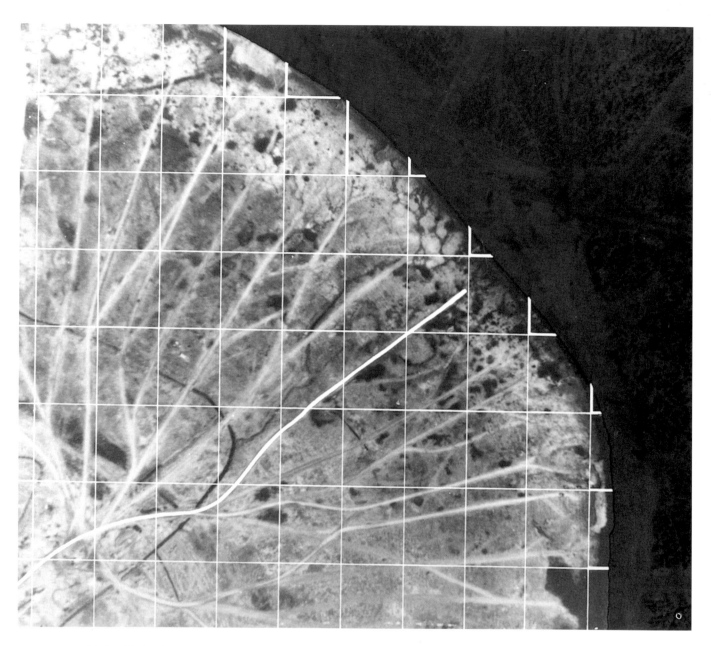

Detail, aerial view of quarry

View of quarry with superimposed grid

Building Measure

February–April 1990

A will which does not issue in a bodily movement and through it in a change in the world totters on the verge of becoming lost in sterile wishing and dreams.

—Paul Ricoeur, *The Voluntary and the Involuntary*

Work by Dan Hoffman with members of the University of Waterloo School of Architecture fourth-year studio: Adrian Blackwell, Stella Evangelidou, Andrew Frontini, Peter Kurkjian, Andrew Power, Katherine Rubinyi, Eric Stedman, Mike Szabo, Andrew Verhiel, Dave Warne, John Willmot, and Tracey Winton

The effort in this investigation was to determine ways in which the body engages in acts of building. This is significant in contemporary architecture because of the increasing use of techniques that distance the body from a direct connection to the building process. Though the efficiencies made available through technological means continue to transform building, we must consider both the knowledge lost in this development and the implications of this loss for an architect's experience.

These questions have come relatively late to building construction, which despite advances in technological production in other areas, remains a labor-intensive activity. This is due in part to the scale and diversity of the tasks required to construct a building and in part to the unique demands presented by each program and site. As a result, buildings are still marked by the body, from hand-lain brick to plywood.

How can the architect remain in contact with physical aspects of the building process? Current standards of professional practice make it clear that the means and methods of erecting a building are the responsibility of the contractor or builder, not the architect, whose role is instead to represent the building in drawings and other documents and to determine the geometric and legal frameworks within which the building is to be constructed. As a result, architects increasingly emphasize means of representation in their work, rather than the bodily acts involved in the building process.

There is a profound difference between describing a line on a drawing and laying that line upon the earth. The former is a representative gesture constructed in a geometric space. The circumstances of its construction are meant to be transparent to the geometric field that is its primary reference. In building a line on the earth, however, one cannot transcend the physical conditions of the site. Local circumstances must be considered. Tools such as the plumb line, float level, carpenter's square, and transit translate the drawing to the site, connecting the acts of constructing a drawing with

The work in progress at the site. All material shown was salvaged from surrounding factories.

the physical acts of laying out the geometry in space. Technological advances such as computer-aided design and the prefabricated wall system eliminate the necessity for such acts of building measure, displacing the bodily reference and ground for building into an encoded language that already possesses the instructions for its own construction.

For this project, it was decided that these issues could best be studied on a building site rather than in a studio setting. Waterloo, Ontario, is typical of many cities in North America in which the economic base is shifting from heavy manufacturing to information-based industries, leaving ample space and materials for such investigations. It is fitting that the detritus of an older, industrial age be used to examine lost relationships between body and building, since many of the found pieces bear traces of the body in their production. The program for this work was simple: to retrieve discarded industrial fragments and examine their potential use as tools for building. Through this exercise we hoped to retrieve some of the knowledge now being lost, to return the invention of the body to architectural practice, and to reestablish the displaced ground for building activity.

This construction used a curved section of fiberglass as formwork to pour a shallow, concrete dome. The formwork scaffolding and ramp doubled as a support for the fiberglass section, which was lowered after the pour was completed.

A primary source of material was the yard of a factory that made large industrial vessels. This barrel was brought to the site and positioned on an angle according to the interior diagonal of its long axis. The barrel was then filled with sand, which was released into burlap sacks.

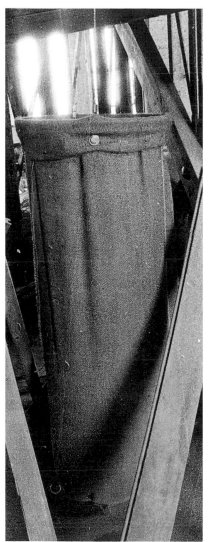

Two participants in the studio carried a large, cylindrically formed steel frame to the site. They thought that the difficulty of this effort should be recorded in the placement of the piece in the site. Through a number of empirical trials it was determined that the frame was twice as heavy as the combined weight of the two carriers. The participants then hung the frame from the ceiling, counterweighted by sandbags equal to the weight of each participant that ran through pulleys attached to the ceiling. To determine the final position of the frame, the sand in the bags was redistributed to reflect the distribution of weight in a horizontal body.

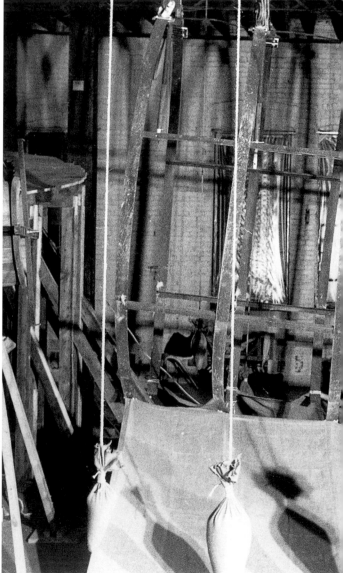

This study began with a large fiberglass funnel. An examination of its movement potential showed that it could evenly distribute gravel placed within it. The participants decided to make a device that would simultaneously form and pour a cylindrical wall. The device would be designed to ride on the top edge of the wall as it increased in height up to eye level, where the pour would end. The complexity of the device was daunting, involving mechanical coordination between the threaded rod that held the diminishing formwork on the rim of the rotating cone and the spiral tracking device that raised the device along its vertical axis. Though the mechanisms were theoretically correct, an oversight in the dimensioning made the device too large, preventing the cone from making a full circle on the track.

During the project a city building inspector arrived at the site and declared that one of the bays of the site was structurally unsound, preventing participants from walking on it. In response, a steel truss member was found and suspended from the columns surrounding the bay, permitting us to cross it without touching the floor. The structure's central support also made the bridge tip like a seesaw when someone walked across it. In addition, a fiberglass trough was also built in along the length of the structure and partially filled with water. When the bridge tipped, the water adjusted to stay level, thereby weighting down the bridge in the direction of the last person to cross.

After the building inspector's visit the group became more conscious of the floor and found that it sloped differently in each bay. To record this condition in an act of building the participants laid one course of brick for each bay on the frame of a moveable dolly. Because of the uneven floor, none of the resulting layers of brick were parallel. However, the last brick course was found to be parallel to the frame of the dolly, making the overall outline of the construction rectangular.

In-between Walls

September 1990–December 1991

Only what is more tightly closed opens.

—Maurice Blanchot, *The Gaze of Orpheus*

Work by David Resnick

The polemics of modern architecture speak of the opening of space and the lightness of structures. The images that we see are filled with a light that sweeps up the shadow in every corner, illuminating with the brightness of day all that has been closed. The interior of architecture has been overcome, all of its darkness compressed into the thickness of a line that separates one exterior from another. Every view is that of a brightly lit surface with another surface behind it. Darkness, where it occurs, simply divides light, the medium of modern space. Modern architecture gives the feeling of space opened, like a fresh book, full of anticipation.

Modern architects gave themselves the task of articulating this open space. They worked to narrow wall sections and to reduce the structures that support and span space. They sought to release the interior energies contained within a volume, to make all space exterior.

Is there not a danger in this singular desire? Will the freshness of an opening and the new beginnings that it allows be lost in the persistent flattening of architecture's interior? What of architects who persist in denying the thickness of the walls that they draw? Is that which exists between walls simply the necessary stuff of building, hidden from the surface by a layer of paint?

"In-between Walls" meditates upon the interior of architecture. It began with the construction of a closed, drywall box suspended in the space of a studio, leaving just enough of a gap between the walls of the studio and the exterior of the box to allow passage. The box displaced the volume of the room to its periphery, transforming the "open" space of the room into space in between walls. This narrow zone became the site of Resnick's further constructions in the space—a concrete column holding a pivot, a piece of plaster bracing the box against rotation, a lead counterweight mounted on the drywall, a rigid foam buffer against the wall—as the box was jostled from one side to another, each movement leaving a trace of its construction. These actions strengthened the closure of the box, for *despite* the manipulations its interior was enhanced. The architect worked directly within the space of construction, in the darkness and confusion that characterize its activity.

As a final action Resnick surprised the viewers by opening the box to reveal an interior. The surprise was compounded by its simple, domestic quality and its quietness relative to the previous, active manipulations of the box. The production of this second interior (the first being the space in between walls) reminded viewers that "only what is more tightly closed opens," that the act of making a closure increases the desire to open. Only when architecture's interior is regained can its opening again be celebrated.

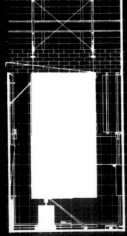

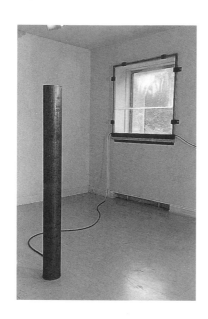

Horizon Level
April–May 1991

Work by Francis Resendes

Perspectival culture views the horizon as an ideal limit-form from which to view and measure constructions. The horizon is always beyond us, out of our reach, and as such lends itself to conceptualization. Like the stars, the horizon locates us relative to our movement on the earth. It is not difficult to understand, then, how the horizon came to be associated with the geometric horizontal, another ideal referent, which anticipates its complement in the orthogonal or vertical angle.

As Michel Serres has noted, time is sacrificed so that space can exist. The horizon exists outside of time; it remains in the same position as we move toward it. To see (conceptually and perceptually) a space beyond the horizon would appear to be impossible since this space would exist outside of any referent, as would a view from beyond and around the horizon toward us, which would see all of our aspects at once. This point of view assumes a total vision, a transparency conceivable only by surpassing vision as we know it. But what if we consider the horizon itself as existing

within us, as particular to our embodied way of being in the world? Can vision and the thinking that it represents respond to a deeper chord?

Francis Resendes's study provokes these questions. Water forms horizon lines in a series of thin, rectangular glass tanks installed over a row of windows of the same size. The tanks are connected by a rubber tube to the bottom of a cylindrical reservoir set at the height of Resendes's eyes. When the reservoir is filled, its level is reproduced in the glass tanks because water always seeks its own level.

Looking through the water level to the horizon beyond alludes to the coincidence of water as a self-leveling material and the idealized geometric horizontal line. This coincidence is weakened, however, at the periphery of our vision where orthogonal lines are warped by the curved structure of the eye, evident when we look at the "dome" of the night sky or at the distant ocean, which curves away from the theoretically straight horizon. Resendes's study indicates that the fluid action of leveling is critical to the formation of the horizon and the horizon idea. This phenomenon operates at both local and global scales. With a fluid level we can position ourselves perpendicular to the earth's surface at a particular point, eliminating the need to refer to the idealization of an abstract horizontal plane.

The phenomenal circuit is complete when we realize that leveling is registered *within* the body in the liquid balance in the cochlear chamber of the ear. The globes of our eyes act as ocular joints between internal and external realms. We externalize this leveling with instruments used to construct buildings. Merleau-Ponty observes: "Our

organs are no longer our instruments, rather our instruments have become our detachable organs."[1] The float level brings the measure of the horizon to construction and, along with the plumb line, transforms the horizontal ideal into real terms. Equipped with this physical understanding we can determine a tangent to the surface of any point on the globe. This geometry is determined by the ever-changing topology of the surface rather than by the fixed idealization of Euclidean geometry's parallel lines. It is important to remember this when we see through the gridded and parallel frames of a contemporary building. The world is not flat, and the horizon is not straight; rather they are part of a continuous surface that curves around upon itself. The body, with its liquid level and motility, makes itself at home on this surface. The perspectival extension to the horizon appears as an act of will born of the desire to fix the limits of the world, making it objectifiable within the abstract frame of a perfected and perfecting representational system.

Notes

1. Maurice Merleau-Ponty, *The Primacy of Perception* (Evanston, Ill.: Northwestern University Press, 1964), 178.

Virtual Opticon

October 1987

Work by James Cathcart

In *Philosophical Investigations* Ludwig Wittgenstein gives a simple demonstration of two uses of the word *see:*

"The one: 'What do you see there?' — 'I see this.'

"(and then a description, a drawing, a copy)

"The other: 'I see a likeness between these two faces.' — Let the man I tell this to be seeing the faces as clearly as I do myself." [1]

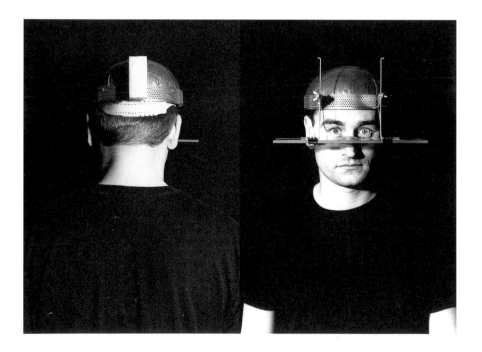

Wittgenstein demonstrates how we use *see* to signify both perceptual ("I see this") and conceptual ("I see a likeness") aspects of vision. The problem is that one meaning is often substituted for the other, thus transforming sight into a symbol of complete and transparent knowledge. To see with both aspects is to see *through* something, to view an object while *seeing* the idea that it represents. To unify these aspects in the light of a rational structure of knowledge has been the heart of our philosophical tradition: to see on both sides of our eyes, to see through the perceptual aspect of vision to the conceptual certainty assumed to lie beyond, a transparent dream where what is thought coincides with what is. Wittgenstein's demonstration shows that the two parts of this unity are preserved in common speech. Two different ways of thinking and describing lodge in the same word.

The architectural conventions of plan, section, and elevation fall into the gap between the objects of sight that Wittgenstein describes. These representations, with their orthogonal or geometric references, offer an impossible point of view located infinitely near or far from the object. We accept these impossible points of view in order to organize an architectural work conceptually. We use them with the unconscious knowledge of tools, their perceptual impossibility fading into the background of convention.

What happens when the gap between the two objects of sight is violated, when a conceptually structured point of view is manifested as a perceptual experience? James Cathcart's "Virtual Opticon" attempts this inversion. It displaces sight from its perceptual focus on the middle ground of the horizon, directing it toward the nearness of the ground below one's feet or the abstract distance of the sky above. The edge of a rectangle of glass rests before the eye in such a way that it presents the sky or the ground, depending on the angle to which it is set. The disorienting ninety-degree shift in perception demonstrates the difficulty in crossing from one manner of seeing to the other. Wearing the device is like inhabiting another world, one in which there is no distance, in which everything collapses between that which is impossibly near or far. The conventions of architectural representation perform the same manipulations, though through use we have become unconscious of their effects. The "Virtual Opticon" reminds us that the body has an orientation and that the "unity" of vision remains an idea, not a reality.

Notes

1. Ludwig Wittgenstein, *Philosophical Investigations* (New York: Macmillan, 1968), 193.

Vision Without Inversion

July–August 1991

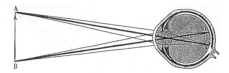

Work by Dan Hoffman with Chris Bauer, Irit Mintz, and Scott Neiswander

In *The Phenomenology of Perception* Merleau-Ponty refers to an experiment entitled "Vision Without Inversion." The experiment is based upon the phenomenon of retinal inversion, whereby the retina receives an inverted visual image from the lens of the eye. We perceive this inverted image as normal, or right side up. In the experiment a subject wears a pair of modified glasses designed to present the retina with an image that is right

side up. The subject therefore perceives the image as being upside down or inverted. The experiment records the subject's impressions. Over a few days the image of the world slowly begins to right itself, despite the glasses. Merleau-Ponty explains this normalization of vision thus: Sight, like any other perception, cannot be isolated from the context of the body and its world. When the subject engages in typical bodily acts, the presence of the feet on the ground and the myriad other contacts with the world compensate for the disturbed function. Being maintains itself as whole: "I already live in the landscape, I see it accordingly as upright, the disturbance brought about by the experiment being concentrated in my own body, which thus becomes, not a mass of affective sensations, but a body which is needed to perceive a given spectacle. Everything throws back onto the organic relations between subject and space, onto that gearing of subject onto his world which is the origin of space."[1]

What has been released in this simple unraveling of the mechanics of vision? The axes of vision and gravity together constitute a conscious, sentient being inevitably "throw[n] back onto the organic relations between subject and space." This simple device temporarily ruptures the field of being, for which the gyroscopic stability of the lived body compensates. We thus glimpse the structure of our being and its relation to the world. A brief understanding of the condition of our ground, which seeks to maintain its structure through embodied experience, results.

The studies presented here attempt to inhabit the horizon of "vision without inversion," to reverse the body's compression-tension axis by inverting loads along the vertical axis. Simply put, a construction inhabited by the body in a number of postures reverses the position of ceiling and floor. The simple logic of inversion belies the physical difficulty of accomplishing this task. How is the body to be inverted? Where will the counterweight be found? Does the body support itself in tension as it does in compression? Perhaps through the physical and pragmatic response to such questions we come to understand our embodied consciousness.

This work also offers the possibility that our vision can release us from the imperative of gravity, providing an internal fulcrum around which the loads of compression may be opposed and reversed. A building is then a sign of the forces deployed to lift it into place. In contemplating a masonry wall can we not ask ourselves how the blocks were stacked by considering the tensile forces that lifted each block into place? To read a structure in this way is to return to its means of construction and the myriad acts and efforts that put it in place.

We glimpse these forces when we place the visual axis parallel to that of gravity, as demonstrated here. This flattens the visual horizon and renders it as a field of force. The body then registers not only the proportional distance from the camera lens but the effect of the forces placed on it. The acceleration toward the horizon implicit in perspective becomes the acceleration due to gravity or its opposite, the acceleration of the ascending force. Here the two ordinates of architectural representation, plan and elevation, combine in a single expression, a vertical plan that registers the possibility of its own extension into building.

Notes

1. Maurice Merleau-Ponty, *The Phenomenology of Perception* (London: Routledge, 1961), 252.

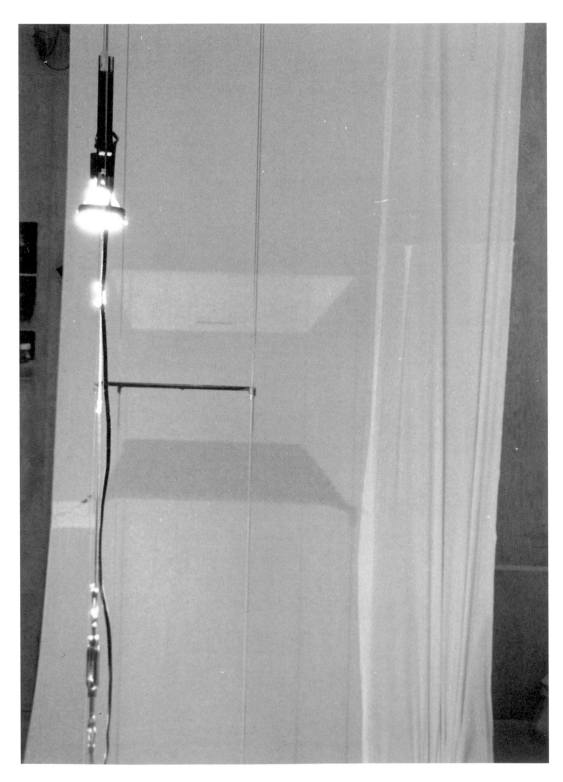

Mirror reflection and shadow

Seeing Double

October 1991–May 1992

Work by Adam Womelsdorf

Italo Calvino writes of a city named Valdrada built on the shores of a lake. The city is built up vertically so that all of its dwellings are reflected in the lake as another Valdrada. Calvino observes: "Nothing exists or happens in the one Valdrada that the other Valdrada does not repeat,"[1] one city mirroring the other.

The mechanism of the mirror attracts us because we are beings that see and are seen, but this does not mean that the two points of view are equal reflections of each other. Merleau-Ponty points out that there is a difference between the "sensing and the sensible"[2] that is lived in the form of a human body. To separate the two is to deny the enigma at the core of our consciousness. The mirror short-circuits this gap between them.

In Valdrada, "inhabitants know that each of their actions is, at once, that action and its mirror-image."[3] All acts in this city are therefore conscious. This does not increase their meaning or significance, however, since all actions are verified only by images of themselves.

We may be more drawn to mirrors when they are invisible or when something caught within them is not duplicated in the world. In Velásquez's *Las Meniñas,* the subjects of the painting look out at us as if they were looking into a mirror. Looking at the painting we too are caught in its reflection. We might speak of this as a reflection of the second degree, whose source is concealed from view and maybe from understanding.

The two Valdradas do not have the luxury of such mysteries. Their inhabitants are caught in their reflections (though Calvino is careful to point out that they are not symmetrical since left is right and right is left in a reflection). "The two Valdradas live for each other, their eyes interlocked; but there is no love between them."[4] By looking into each other's eyes, the inhabitants of Valdrada lock in an embrace with their own image. Such is the attraction and danger of mirrors.

Notes

1. Italo Calvino, *Invisible Cities* (San Diego: Harcourt Brace Jovanovich, 1974), 53.

2. Maurice Merleau-Ponty, *The Primacy of Perception* (Evanston, Ill.: Northwestern University Press, 1964), 168.

3. Calvino, *Invisible Cities*, 53.

4. Calvino, *Invisible Cities*, 54.

Tension/compression-concrete reflection

Window reflection

Earth-Ark

January–April 1993

The earth is the ark which makes possible in the first place the sense of all motion and all rest as a mode of motion. But its rest is not a mode of motion.

—Edmund Husserl, "Origin of the Spatiality of Nature"

Work by Theodore Galante

With the rise of the Copernican worldview, in which the earth is a body among other bodies moving in space, the earth was displaced from its position as the stable referent for the movement of celestial bodies. This new relativism could theoretically be extended to infinity, making our location in space just one of an infinitude of possible locations and our movement part of an infinitude of movements.

Husserl observes, however, that it is a mistake to assume that the nature described by modern Copernican science is the same as that which we experience when we describe our own relationship to the earth. This nature, or earth, he states, "comes about as a synthetic unity in a manner analogous to the way in which the experiential fields of a single person are unified in continuous and combined experience."[1] Just as the ego as an embodied consciousness unifies experience, providing a referent through which we orient ourselves among others, the idea of *earth* orients our sense of boundaries in nature and our place within it.

When we consider the earth as simply a body among other bodies, we deny the manner in which we orient ourselves not only in space but within our own history. In physical terms, the movement of a body is always with reference to a "basis-body," as the movement of a ball is with reference to the ground. Though we can also conceive of the earth as a moving body in the cosmos, for the moment that we see the ball in motion, the earth seems still. Our sense of the motion of the ball depends upon it. Our experience of time also works through memories, which function in a like manner

as stable referents with which to note time's passage. These memories also accumulate in a history and point back to a primal referent or origin, as vague and distant as it may be, a home base that makes possible our movement through time.

Ted Galante's studies of motion demonstrate the unease we feel when the earth-ark reference is subverted. In the first exercise, a large sheet of glass is placed upon a horizontal track fixed to the floor. Attached to the track and supporting the glass are a number of evenly placed rubber wheels, which permit the glass to be moved back and forth. The movement is slow and silent; the glass reflects the ceiling above as it moves. If one fixes one's eyes on the glass, however, one has the curious sensation that the glass is still and the floor is moving—a sensation similar to that of sitting in a motionless train in a station and seeing the station platform begin to "move." This initial feeling reveals the unconscious structures upon which we orient ourselves relative to motion. The experience of a Copernican world would be much the same, with us constantly attempting to recover a primary spatial and temporal orientation.

The second piece builds on the slipping action of the first by adding a rotating vertical component, a map mounted on rollers that can be viewed through a horizontal slot. Here the motion occurs on two axes, compounding the difficulty of establishing a stable reference in order to read the map. (The map is Piranesi's of the Campo Marzio, whose buildings and monuments also float on a destabilized field.)

The double slippage demonstrates the precariousness and disorientation we feel when the earth-reference is unhinged from its mooring as a primary referent. Movement along this double axis can be likened to inhabiting the trajectory of a scientist's dream. Husserl reminds us, however, that we always wake up to find the earth at our feet.

Notes

1. Edmund Husserl, "Origin of the Spatiality of Nature," in *Husserl: Shorter Works* (South Bend, Ind.: University of Notre Dame Press, 1981), 223.

"Earth-Ark" study (glass on rollers)

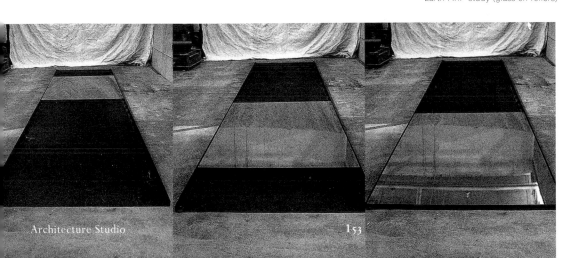

Simultaneous movement along two axes

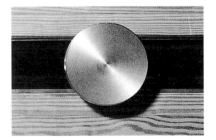

Bearing detail from "Earth-Ark"

Tomb

November 1991

Man is made in his own image: this is what we learn from the strangeness of the resemblance of cadavers. But this formula should first of all be understood this way: <u>man is unmade according to his image.</u>

—Maurice Blanchot, *The Gaze of Orpheus*

Work by Jonathan Rader

There is something of a death in the desire to reduce the figure to a resemblance of itself and to transform an immaterial image into the hardness of a solid body. The tradition of classical art and architecture rests upon this double negation that establishes a connection between the body and its ideal image. As Blanchot concludes: "Thus art was at once ideal and true, faithful to the figure and faithful to the truth that admits of no figure."[1]

The tomb is the form where the traditions of classical art and architecture intersect; in the space of death the dual aspects of resemblance and truth maintain their uncanny equation. On entering a tomb we believe that we are in the presence of a dead body, a place where the image of death is given a material face. Deprived of the view of the body itself, we seek its evidence in the forms of the tomb. The architecture of the tomb derives both from this latent expectation of an encounter and from the realization that the idealized form from which the tomb is constructed can never yield a "true" likeness of the absent body. We accept this sacrifice of the image in order to maintain its memory. Geometry and its forms are imbued with this sacrifice, which transforms them into sacred vessels. These, in their ideal state, maintain an image of the body over time.

Rader's project weighs these themes of death and resemblance, considering not only the image of the absent body but the manner in which forms are produced and made present. In this case, Rader constructed the image by imprinting his body in a bed of wet concrete. This process was carefully documented through a series of photographs beginning with the construction of a rectangular formwork to contain the concrete. Once the bed was poured and lain upon, a second layer was poured over the first, producing a positive impression of the body that was partially revealed when the two pours were separated. A glance into the horizontal reveal between the two sections does not offer an immediately recognizable image but conveys the distinct sense that the distended form within was touched by the body—if it is not the body itself. The sense of the body's presence prevails over the brute evidence of the construction's concrete, material process. The desire to discover the image of the body in other places can make and unmake the manner in which we appear to the world.

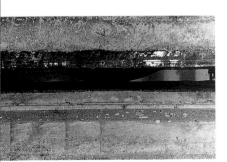

Notes

1. Maurice Blanchot, *The Gaze of Orpheus* (Barrytown, N.Y.: Station Hill, 1981), 85.

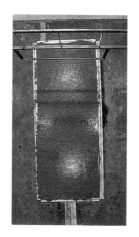

Doll House

August 1993

Work by Sukhwant Jhaj and Jane Martin

This project was an entry to a competition, sponsored by *Art Papers* magazine, to design a doll house.[1] Jhaj and Martin understood the program of the doll house to involve the construction of certain cultural ideals through the activities of play. They provided the following statement as a guide for their work:

Through play, the ideals:

idealized house (doll house)

idealized human (doll)

idealized form (cube).[2]

The project's two components—the list of ideals and the processes by which they were made material—form a dialogue wherein various aspects of the doll house establish oppositions and create a third, critical space within which to view the program. The ideal forms of doll house, doll, and cube appear only as a result of negation of another, parallel form. For example, the space of the doll house exists in the form of the virtual formwork made to cast the plaster. The doll exists as a virtual present as the negative formwork, making the piece an interlocking pair of formed object and empty mold, a double negative out of which the idea(l) of the doll house emerges. Photographs that document the work also vibrate between these negative and positive aspects, creating a curious "other" space within which the forms of the blocks and doll appear.

As children are told, two wrongs do not make a right, but their pairing does form another, third condition when they are set in opposition to each other. Such a structure produces another truth whose ambiguity offers a way out of the oppositions that ideals always produce.

Notes

1. "Doll House," *Art Papers* (Atlanta) 17, no. 5 (September/October 1993): 1.

2. "Doll House," 1.

160

Skin

October 1992–January 1993

Work by Gregory Yang

The work began with the idea of surveying the surface of the body. The method involved photographing the body in small sections perpendicular to the local curve of its surface, thereby unwrapping it onto a flat plane. This process also required that adjacent photographs be cropped along a shared line or contour, since the surface of the body is constituted by compound curves that turn away from the flat picture plane, moving out of focus and distorting scale.[1] The individual pieces, when rejoined along these lines, approximate the body's original curvature, reconstituting its complex surface. This method, however, can never yield a true map of the body, as it requires an infinite number of photographs to flatten the compound curves.

The desire to transform the body into a flat surface might be explained by the parallel desire to leave the body itself. One is reminded here of the "mantle of invisibility" (made of animal skins) worn by Plains Indians warriors to make them invisible to their enemies.[2] Such practices demonstrate that being does not constitute itself entirely within a body; our existence is constituted in part through the gaze of others, to the extent that we feel compelled to shed our own skins.

A survey of one's own skin also produces this feeling of disembodiment. The intense visual scrutiny separates one's self from the body. The self, thus vulnerable, searches for another skin to inhabit. The collages reconfigure pieces of the original mapping into variously distorted bodies. As if the survey had loosened the genetic code that maintains our bodily form, it grows in multiple directions, each limb informed by its own tropism. This "becoming vegetable" also leaves behind the mind and the will: the head becomes just another limb of a seeking, feeding organism that grows within the surrounding, aqueous medium. The skinning produces an organism that cannot survive without being immersed in a supporting medium. These mutations reverse

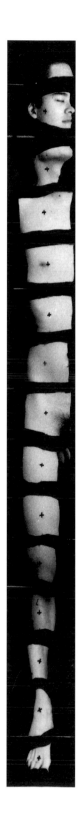

the evolutionary trajectory, returning the body to the crucial moment when it had to choose to eat or be eaten.

The skin of the body is a powerful symbol that, when manipulated, resonates with the structure of being. By operating upon it we unleash the perverse desire to become one with all things. Does this open a hell from which we can never escape, or is it a necessary reckoning with the evolutionary inheritance of which we may be a part?

Notes

1. This process of contour matching was developed by Studio member Chris Kaiser.

2. The term *mantle of invisibility* is used to describe an American Indian hunting cloak in Garrick Mallery's *Picture Writing of the American Indians* (New York: Dover Publications, 1972), vol. 2, 503.

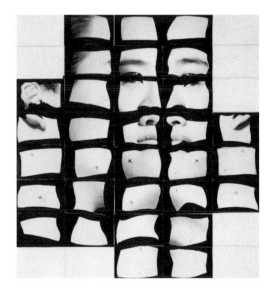

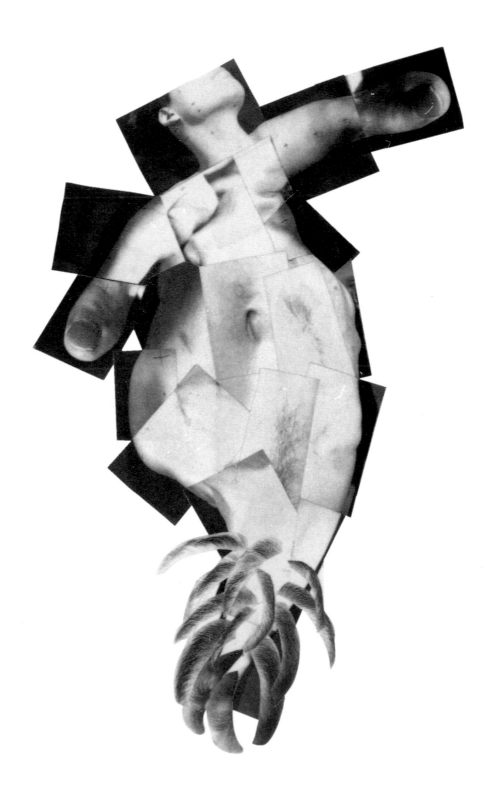

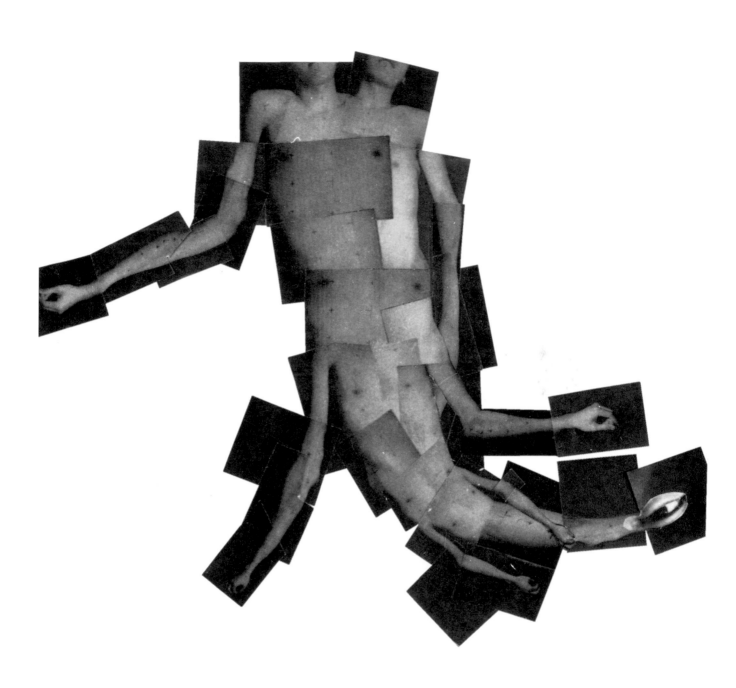

Concrete block wall

Recording Wall
July–August 1991

Work by Dan Hoffman

In "Recording Wall" an eight-by-sixteen-foot concrete block wall was erected without mortar. Each block was photographed as it was put in place. (Cameras on both sides of the wall were activated by an extended shutter release located near the builder's foot.) The photographs were then printed on the surface of each block using a liquid photo emulsion and the wall was reassembled in its original order.

The resulting wall became a literal recording of its own construction or deconstruction, the photographs offering a supplemental reading that recorded the postural effort required to build it. This mediated layer restored the sign of a bodily activity to the assembly of industrially produced masonry units, a reading often lost in considering contemporary architecture. A closer reading evokes the repetitive, Sisyphean labors involved in building and unbuilding the wall and reminds us that building is an embodied task. Modernism's utopian vision erases the mark of this toil in the work. But before we accept this erasure, we should recall Camus's meditation on Sisyphus, which shows the depth of being that can exist in a simple, repetitive task. Camus writes of the moment when Sisyphus turns to follow the rock that has once again tumbled down to the bottom of the hill:

"It is during that return, that pause, that Sisyphus interests me. A face that toils so close to stones is already stone itself! I see that man going back down with a heavy yet measured step toward the torment of which he will never know the end. That hour like a breathing space which returns as surely as his suffering, that is the hour of consciousness. At each of those moments when he leaves his heights and gradually shrinks toward the lair of the gods, he is superior to his fate. He is stronger than his rock." [1]

Notes

1. Albert Camus, *The Myth of Sisyphus and Other Essays* (New York: Random House, 1955), 89.

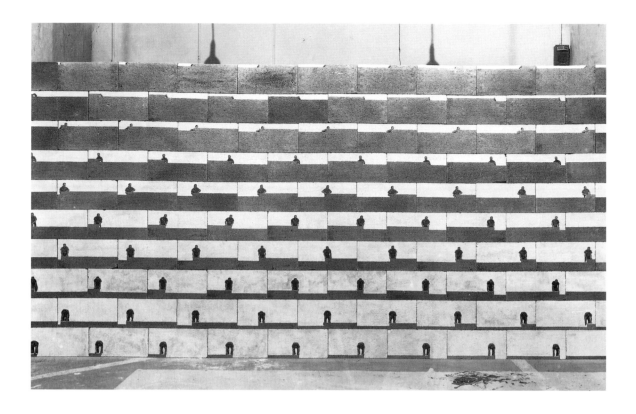

Concrete block wall with superimposed photographs

Individual concrete blocks with superimposed photographs

Sample of the brickwork
at Cranbrook

Unwrapped blueprint of expanded brick pile

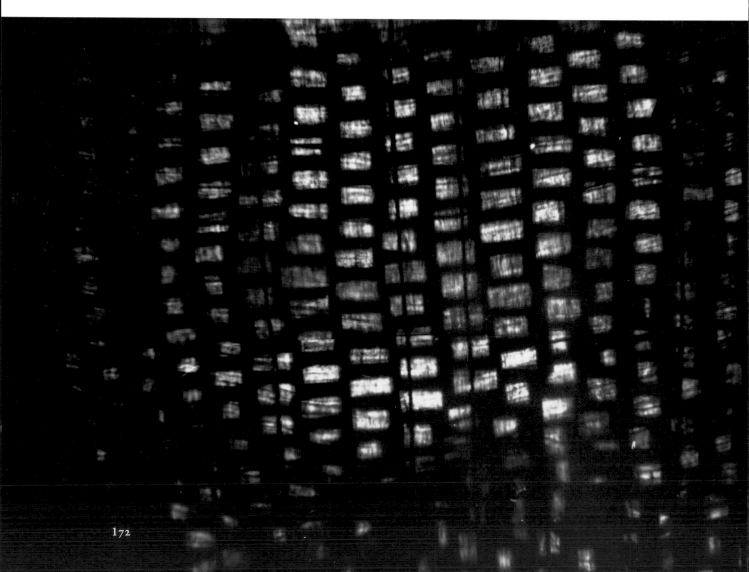

Brick-Fabric
January–March 1993

Work by Alfred Zollinger

One distinctive aspect of the architecture at Cranbrook is highly textured brick walls. Eliel Saarinen took great care in detailing the brick for his designs, using all manner of patterns and sizes so that the wall became a virtual fabric of brick. In speaking about these walls he often referred to the brick wall as a tapestry, using the work of his wife, the weaver Loja Saarinen, as an inspiration. At Cranbrook material processes typical of certain artistic disciplines are crossbred with other processes to produce remarkable hybrids. The activities of production support each other by extending their reach and providing new territories for creative work.

In this piece by Alfred Zollinger the relationship between masonry and fabric is studied through the transformation of a pile of bricks into a thin, diaphanous wall. This occurs in a number of steps. First the bricks are made into a compact, rectangular pile; then they are displaced toward the periphery of the pile to create a large, interior volume that is square at the base and round at the top. Surrounding the expanded volume is a large sack of burlap which acts as a tension ring for the construction, stiffening the coursing rings of brick. The work was performed from the interior of the pile, which required that a ladder be built in to exit the construction. Recordings of the wall were produced by wrapping the exterior with blueprint paper. The prints were then hung on a wall as the final unwrapping of the brick solid.

The transformation of the darkness of brick into a tissue of light embodies the mystery of architectural construction. Saarinen understood that such mysteries are worked out in an environment thick with the knowledge of material techniques. It is just this environment that the Architecture Studio seeks to maintain.

Original brick pile

Brick pile wrapped in burlap

View inside extruded burlap wrapping

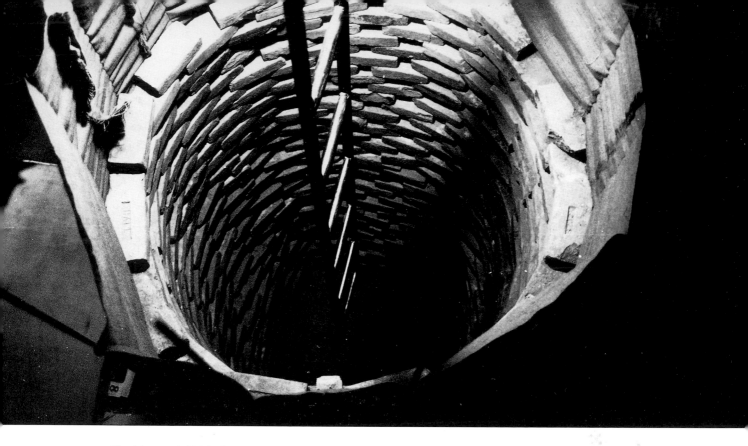

View into expanded brick pile wrapped in burlap

176

View of expanded brick pile wrapped in burlap

Hay Stack
January 1993

Work by the Architecture Studio with members of the University of Toronto School of Architecture and Landscape Architecture fifth-year studio: Jose Castel-Branco, Elaine Didyk, Tom Kyle, Anita Matusevics, Shannon McGaw, Michael Rietta, Steve Suchy, and Jonathan Winton

In 1938 Eliel Saarinen designed a library and museum for the Cranbrook Academy of Art. This was the last in a string of buildings that Saarinen had designed for the Academy, the earliest being a 1925 structure, typical of the Northern European Romanesque, housing artists' studios. The change from the early buildings to the library and museum complex indicates the transformation in Saarinen's thinking about design and fabrication. In the first buildings he paid great attention to craft, in particular to traditional brick patterns and details. The buildings have a distinctly hand-hewn appearance appropriate to the arts-and-crafts sensibility dominant at the time at Cranbrook. The library and museum addition and its distinctive peristyle, despite careful detailing and sculptural appointments, are a far cry from the humble and localized attitudes toward craft and community represented by the earlier buildings. It is said that all dreams of power lead to Rome, and with its reduced, classical sensibility, the peristyle in particular symbolizes Saarinen and the Academy's more "international" aspirations.

We at the Cranbrook Architecture Studio have always been impressed by the quiet beauty and proportional rigor of the peristyle but remain wary of the universalizing aspects of its design. It is our feeling that Saarinen drifted a bit too far from Ruskin's dictum to "keep your hands on the plough"; this architecture begins to turn its back on handwork and the proximity of the architect to the building process. Dreams of power are dreams of distance, great distance that demands high levels of organization and control.

In order to infuse the peristyle with the qualities of the early buildings, the Studio wrapped its columns with bales of hay. Here again one sees the effort of putting each piece of a building into place, giving the structure a scale indicative of the craft-based traditions to which the early structures of Cranbrook aspired.

The machine shown at the left illustrates the rigid yet trim construction of the 18" and 22" carriage Burroughs Typewriters. Because of the electric carriage return and electric shift to capitals, these typewriters are as easy to operate as a narrow carriage typewriter.

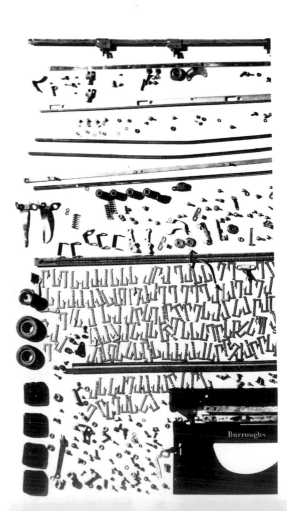

1935 Burroughs Typewriter

October 1990

Device: A thing that is made, usually for a working purpose.

—The Random House Dictionary of the English Language

Work by Jonathan Rader

The root of the word *device* is the Middle English "devis," meaning both division and discourse. The word's dual aspect indicates that a device entails two forms of analysis: the abstract or logical form that divides a purpose into its constituent parts, and the discursive form that establishes the purpose within the frame of human affairs. If we intend to make something for a specific, working purpose we must divide or analyze aspects of the task at hand so that we may focus our activities. The purpose of a device is to make things work, to set things in motion toward an end.

The Latin root of *device* is the verb *vicere,* meaning to turn. This reading is consistent with the idea that a device sets things in motion or, to be more specific, sets them turning. The prefix *de-* indicates a counter motion, however. Understood in this way, a device can mean an un turning or re-turning, an active taking apart that makes the movement of turning possible.

Architecture Studio

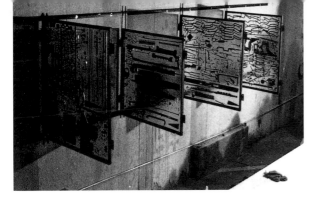

Typewriter parts embedded in a book of
hinged resin wall panels

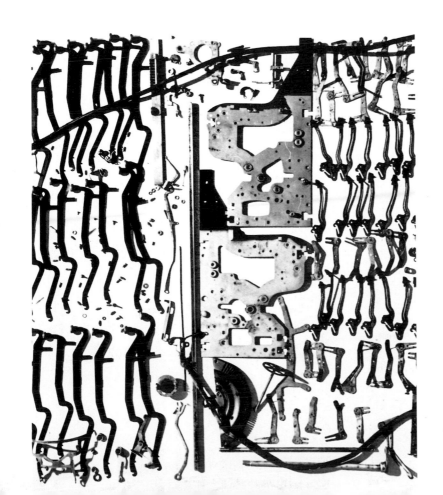

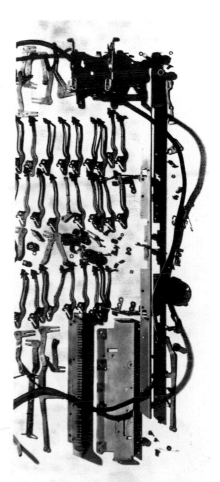

Work by Jeanine Centuori

The Architecture Studio persists in believing that the processes used to manipulate material can both inspire and manifest an architectural pursuit. Though material processes are necessary to construct buildings, much of our work is devoted to ways in which these processes can carry and intensify architectural ideas.

Flattened Room
January–May 1991

Jeanine Centuori investigates the potential of latex rubber to record topological or multidimensional surfaces of objects. This material can be applied in a liquid state to complex surfaces, becoming, as it dries, an elastic skin. This can then be peeled off and flattened to reveal the continuous, developed surface. As a liquid, latex can cover surfaces that would be impossible to describe with conventional, orthographic drawing, enabling us to think *around* objects rather than through the two-dimensional cuts of a section or the flat projection of an elevation.

The site for this project was a table setting for a meal in a room within the architecture studio. Each item in the room was covered with latex and then unwrapped onto six four-by-eight-foot panels in the order that they were covered. The unwrapping was done in a manner particular to each object: radial patterns for circles, orthogonal patterns for rectangular forms, and so on. The resulting picture is unpredictable yet curiously familiar. It is as if the flattened skins were waiting for a breath of volume to peel themselves off the panel and be reconfigured, their surfaces carrying the memory of the original volumes. We sense their potential to occupy volumetric space and unconsciously fill them. They recall John Hejduk's masque objects, whose distinctive profiles flatten dimensions like shadows on the ground, volumes that carry the ghost of their drawings around with them; however, in Centuori's project the volumes themselves are the ghosts.

Though the flattened skins could be described as representations of the original objects, their material presence offers something more in the evidence, or trace, of the material and processes involved. Unanticipated details are picked up in places which offer a texture of readings in addition to the geometry involved in re-forming the objects. For example, the difficulty of a particular detail or pattern an object leaves upon the surface gives a temporal and material dimension to the work.

A running description of the objects in the room, written by Centuori, accompanies the flattened objects, thereby providing an additional reading of the piece. The combination of image and text offers a structure similar to that of a musical score, enabling us to reinhabit the room within the space of multiple interpretations.

In the center of the room, there is a table. The table is made of a wooden top which is white, or at least the very top layer is white. It's a thin layer of paint which is very worn. There are a lot of scratches and marks on it. It appears to have been worked on quite a bit, mostly with a sharp object. On the table there are several objects which are mostly dishes. On the table, furthest to the right of the chair, is a small white porcelain dish with an insignia on it that says *Ford* in gray script letters. Just in front of the dish, a little bit to the left, there is a green wine bottle. Just to the left of the small Ford dish there is a silver spoon, a soup spoon. To the top or

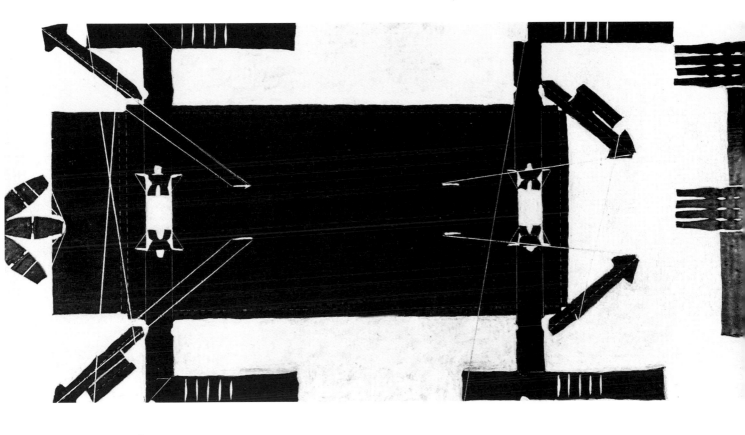

front of that is a glass which is empty, and it appears as though it could hold about eight ounces of liquid. At the very left of the knife, there is a large dinner plate; it's an off-white porcelain dish. To the left of the plate there is a napkin, which is really a paper towel. Sitting on the paper towel is a fork whose design seems to almost match the knife and spoon. To the top, or toward the front, of the fork and napkin there is a jar, a glass jar with a white lid which is tightly closed down around the jar. To the left, almost near the edge of the table, is a glass bowl with a spoon in it. The underside of the table is bare wood which is quite splintery,

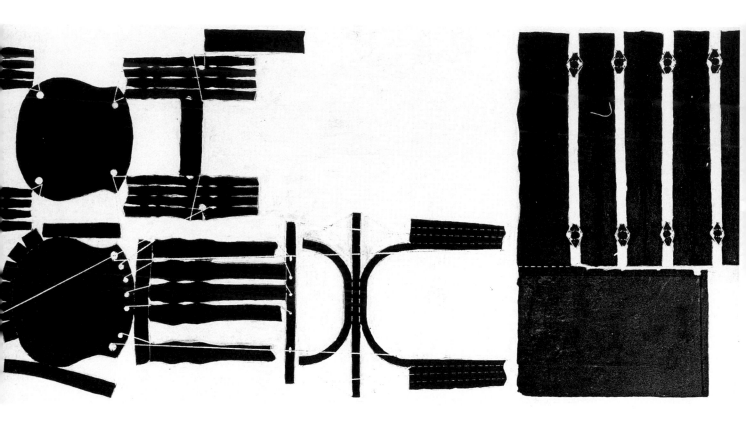

and it has a lot of knots in it which are depressions in the surface. The supports of the table are metal, and seem to have been put there by hand. The table contacts the floor at four points, and there is a black rubber stopper at each of the points. Along the long side of the table, and near the dinner plate, there is a wooden chair, which is slightly tilted out from the table as though someone had just left. There are four legs which are seemingly identical, except for their angle. Behind the chair to its left, if you were sitting in it, is a chest of drawers. It sits in the corner of the room, touching three of its surfaces. The frontmost object on the chest

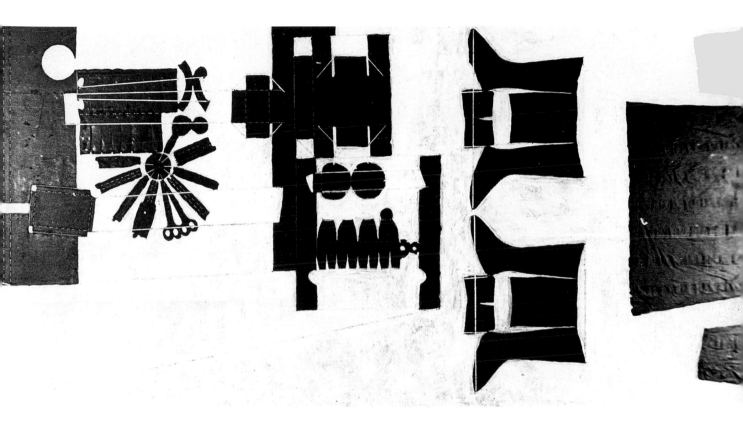

of drawers is a book, a small red book, with the title *Waste.* On the very right side of the chest of drawers, almost near the right edge, there is a porcelain cup which is white with a blue image on it. The picture is a bucolic scene with a windmill, a body of water, a boat, a tree, and a house. Around the edge of the image there is a scrolling line that frames it. In the mug are some objects, mostly pencils, a scissor, erasers, and some odd implements. To the left of the mug, there is a plain wooden rectangular box with a white-and-blue ceramic inlay in its top. Behind this box there is another wooden box. Its top is obscured by a third box. This last

box is a blondish wood with a metal clasp at the front. On top of it is a very ornate wooden box which appears to open on a hinge. To the left of the two boxes there is a pink alarm clock with the image of the globe on its face. On the left of the alarm clock there is a small green porcelain cup. The side of the dresser is a brown wood, also painted, and appears to be the same color as the top, although the side is not as worn as the top. At the very base of the chest of drawers, next to its side, there is an outlet, or extension cord, which has a brown plug in it. The extension cord disappears behind the chest of drawers. There is another white extension cord coming out of the first cord, and going up and away from it. To the very left of the chest of drawers, on the floor, is a pair of

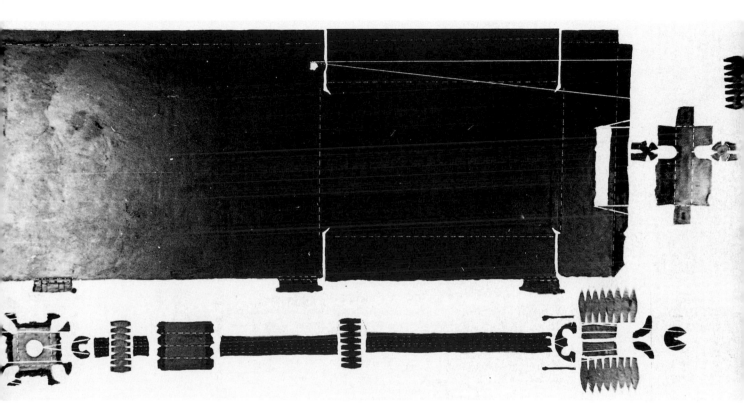

black rubber boots. Above the boots, hanging on the wall at about eye level, there is a jacket. It's plaid and very colorful. The purple and the red are very distinct large lines, and the areas filled in-between are green and brown. Just to the left of the jacket, attached to a pipe running on the wall, is a lamp which has a clamp connector with rubber ends that holds itself on the pipe with pressure. The cord attached to this lamp is connected to the extension cord on the floor, which continues to connect another lamp located on the other side of the table. It's a tall, thin floor lamp, which is made of metal and marbled glass pieces. At the opposite corner, next to the clamp lamp, there is a door which is connected to the walls of the room.

Space-Enfolding-Breath

September 1992–April 1993

Work by Monica Wyatt

Monica Wyatt began her work with a list of questions, noted in her thesis, in search of a definition of a wall:

To define a wall: What is a wall?

Is a wall defined by its thickness, height, and resistance to penetration?

Is a wall measurable, finite, with two sides, this side and the other?

Is a wall defined by what occurs on the other side?

Is a wall an object such as myself with space separating us?

Can I be (in) a wall, fixed and watching bodies move with space separating us?

Can a wall be merely the surface with which one comes in contact, with the substance behind/beyond the surface as something else?

Can I define a wall considering only the frontal relationships, just one of the surfaces? Is a wall the surface with which I am immediately confronted?

(Can the wall be that which always separates me from the other object? Is space the medium that always separates, or does it merely fill the gap that is impassable?)

The questions are phenomenological and psychological, attempting to account not only for the physical presence of the wall itself but for how it is there for *her*. Like Wyatt's own body, walls have fronts and backs, interiors and exteriors. They can separate and bind, and they also possess the point of view of an other from which one is viewed. For Wyatt the wall is ambiguous: even though it presents itself as a physical limit to her body, it provokes the desire to move beyond its bounds. Her confessed desire is to "get into the wall," to escape from the physical limits of the surroundings so that she may see herself from the other side. Wyatt desires to be simultaneously in both places, impossible if one accepts the materialist proposition that two bodies cannot occupy the same space at the same time. She desires, however, to make this possible, to conceive of a situation in which space and material become intertwined, as if consciousness and body were intertwined within the space of a fold.

This project documents Wyatt's search, starting with simple folding operations performed with thin sheets of lead and ending with the surface of the wall being transformed into the skin of the body. In the end Wyatt entered the wall through a logic that allows for multiple faces of consciousness. It is possible to occupy a wall only if we accept that we are present for others as well as for ourselves. By projecting ourselves into another's point of view, we construct a space within which being is defined and constituted.

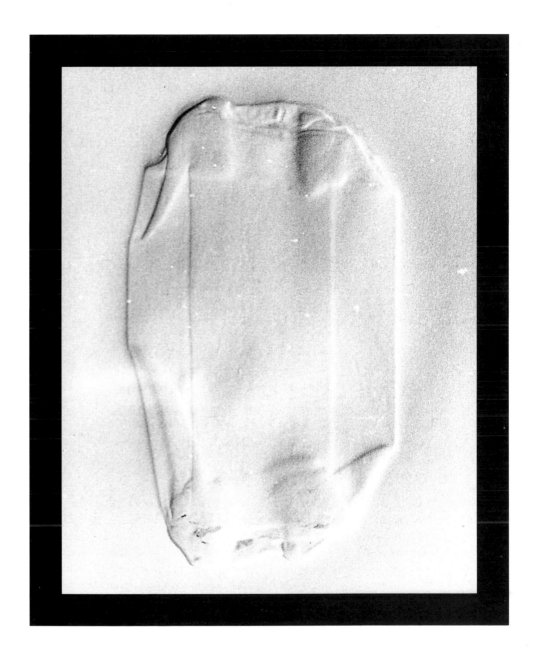

Pressed-Brick Wrappings The effort to enter the wall began with the idea that
a wall must have space within it to be entered. Monica Wyatt constructed this "space"
symbolically by wrapping a brick in lead sheet and extracting the brick. She then
flattened the brick wrapping by running it through a printing press. Though flat, the
print of the collapsed brick bears the traces of its former volume, and though the
interior is not physically accessible, one feels that its space has come to the surface.
Here the flattened lead wrapping is impressed on soft, white paper.

Cruciform Folding These prints are from a series of foldings performed on a cruciform-shaped lead sheet. One image shows the interior side of the lead pressing through to the visible surface. Wyatt states: "In my prints the surface alludes to spaces seemingly hidden inside—insides made by folding, originally on the outside, pressed to the inside, with a new surface created. The skin is malleable; the surface can be unfolded exposing the 'inside' but with a permanent alteration in shape. This is the persistence of past actions, transformations."

The fold is the key, for within this action the exterior is brought to the interior. With the second action of enfolding there exists the possibility of having the interior reappear on the exterior.

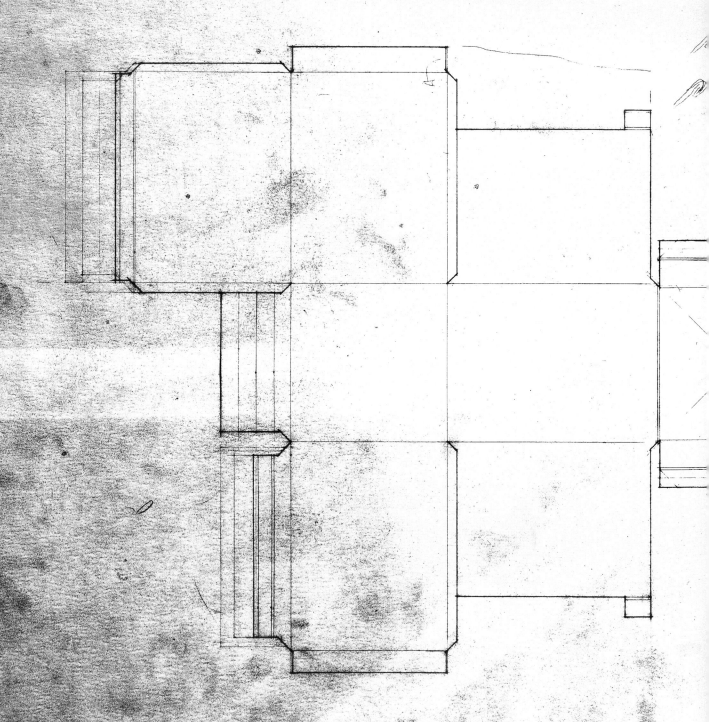

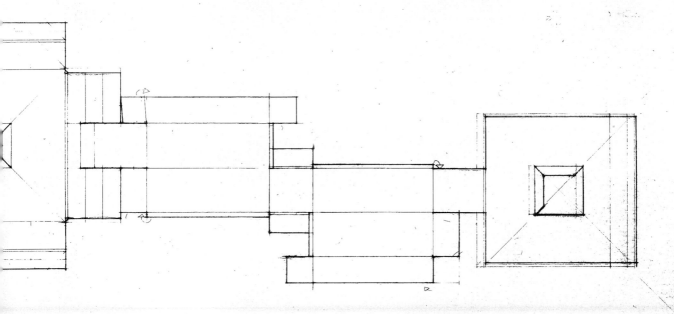

Lead Box Plans The problem here was to produce a box from a single piece of lead. The process of folding was not to be planned in advance; the plan was to result from the construction process. Wyatt established the following operating rules:

The plan is constructed on a single piece of material.

No raw edges may show.

Excess is good; it can represent density, create structure, allow for expansion.

Each material requires a different plan; though the difference may be small, the rules of construction follow the properties of the material and its possible everyday use.

Everything must follow a logic, whether fictional or not.

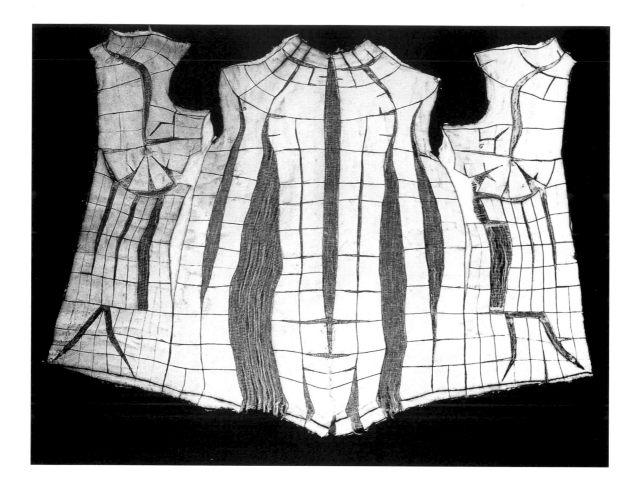

Planning the Body Through the operation of the fold a flat continuous surface can be developed into a body. The task again is to develop a plan.

The body itself presents certain difficulties. Its surfaces are continuous and pliable and constantly change with movement. Planning such a surface requires a material that can come in direct contact with the skin itself. Liquid latex rubber conforms precisely to the surface that it touches. As it dries, it must accommodate bodily movements such as the expansion of the rib cage during breathing. Here the plan pattern was cut and filled with enough cotton gauze to accommodate this expansion. This extra space allowed the body to slip out of the skin.

Inhabiting the Wall Once the plan was produced, it was used to cut out a pattern on a wall covered with wallpaper. The resulting shape was peeled off the wall and made into the form of the body from which it was drawn, its pleats gathered and held with snaps. By putting on the body-dress, Wyatt was able to gather the interior surface of the wall around her, fulfilling her desire to "be in the wall."

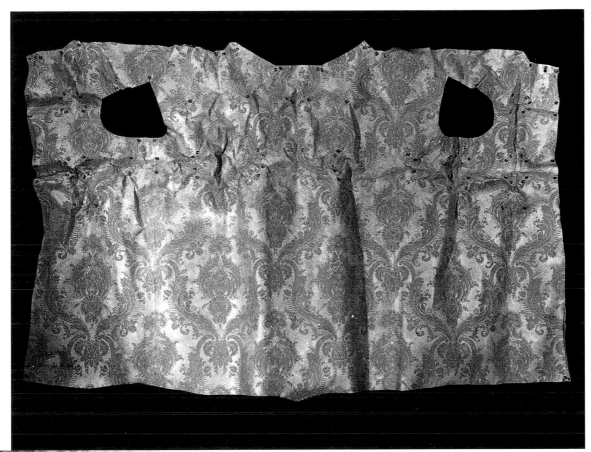

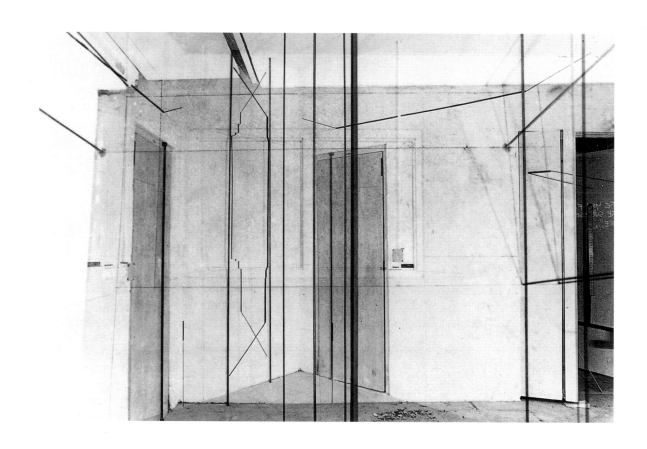

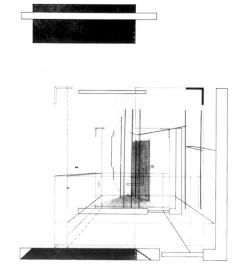

Drawing in the Space of Construction

January–April 1992

Work by Kamol Jangkamolkulchai

In the story "Of Exactitude in Science," Borges describes an empire obsessed with the idea of mapping its extent. The maps become increasingly complex, as more and more of its aspects are recorded, growing until the empire becomes a map of itself.[1] Though Borges does not describe how the map empire was constructed, we assume that its surface is covered with symbols, with every object a representation of itself. The plans, sections, and elevations of buildings, for example, would appear as full-scale representations. Borges notes that the impossible empire no longer exists, but we can understand the mapmakers' desire that the map itself become reality, passing over the difficult and unpredictable aspects of material construction. When the map or drawing becomes the thing-in-itself, the vectors of body and abstraction cross and all material is transparent to mind. There are no interiors, no opacities. Every action occurs in a space already mapped out. Every action therefore becomes a construction of the map.

View of the studio

Jangkamolkulchai's drawings appear to offer a glimpse into this realm. They were constructed by drawing on photographs taken with a camera mounted orthographically with respect to the walls and floor of a room in the studio, compressing the perspectival depth between the camera and the surface to a flatness that approaches a plan or elevation. The indexical evidence of the photograph thus serves as a symbolic representation that can be manipulated according to its own two-dimensional rules. The photograph's compressed ground generates further drawings. Lines inscribed on these are then built into the space of the room, setting off another round of photographic mapping. This cycle of photography, drawing, and construction repeats until it is impossible to determine what is material and what is representation. Here the architectural object is brought into spatial and representational ambiguity, a charged field that breaks down the distance and opacity of things.

Notes

1. Jorge Luis Borges, "On Exactitude in Science," *Universal History of Infamy* (New York: Dutton, 1972), 141.

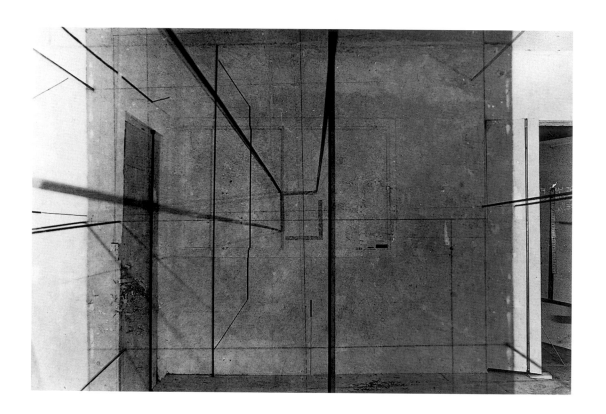

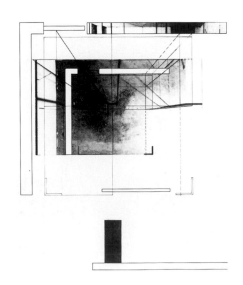

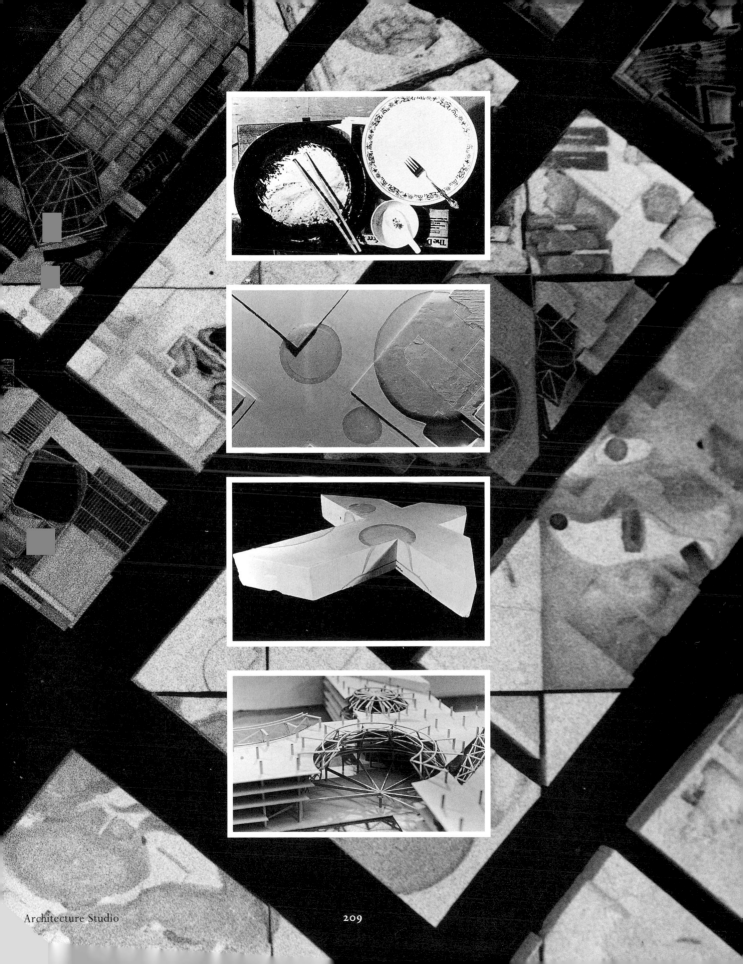

Studio Process

The Studio set itself the problem of finding a shared territory between Borges's map of the empire and the associative memory structure of Proust. The two offer complementary visions of consciousness. An intersection between them suggests the tantalizing possibility of a map of memories, a map infused with time.

The work began with the individual students designating meaningful relationships of personal objects within their own homes, which they were to record and document using photographs and constructive, geometric analyses. After isolating the critical relationships, they reconstructed them in a given space using wood, cloth, and wax. They covered the construction with plaster and organized the individual sections according to a street map of an abandoned neighborhood in Detroit, carving the streets, blocks, and houses into the plaster. All available information on the area, including structures that were no longer standing, went on the map. To articulate the map a correspondence was established between various building conditions and the depth of excavation from the surface. For example, if a house no longer existed on a site, its outline was excavated to a given depth. As the plaster was removed, fragments of submerged objects began to be revealed.

The object/map was then segmented into streets and blocks to show both the excavations on the map and sections through the objects buried below. Students then selected one sectional fragment to examine its potential for building.

They recorded this process through photography and interpreted it through axonometric "memory" drawings that functioned both as temporal projections and as notations of the stages in the project, tracing the transformation of the fragment from object to proto-building within the "archaeological plan" of the site. The combination of indexical means, such as photography and photocopying, and iconographic representations, such as cartography and architectural drawing, allowed us to describe not only what was available to the eye but also what was buried or present in memory, enlarging the dialogue between personal memory and rational construct.

Intertwining

The insertion of the private realm, as represented by familial, personal objects, into the public realm of the city map challenges the traditional hierarchies and boundaries of space and culture. This offers a perspective of the American city represented not only by the forms of "rational" planning but also by the accumulation of objects and associations at a personal, individual scale.

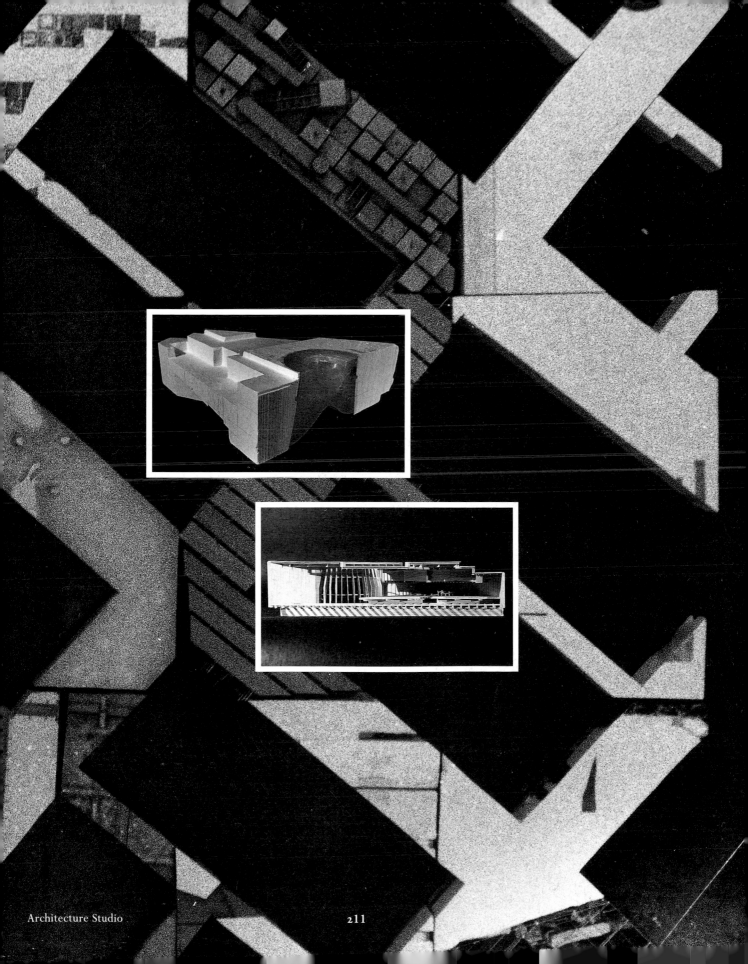

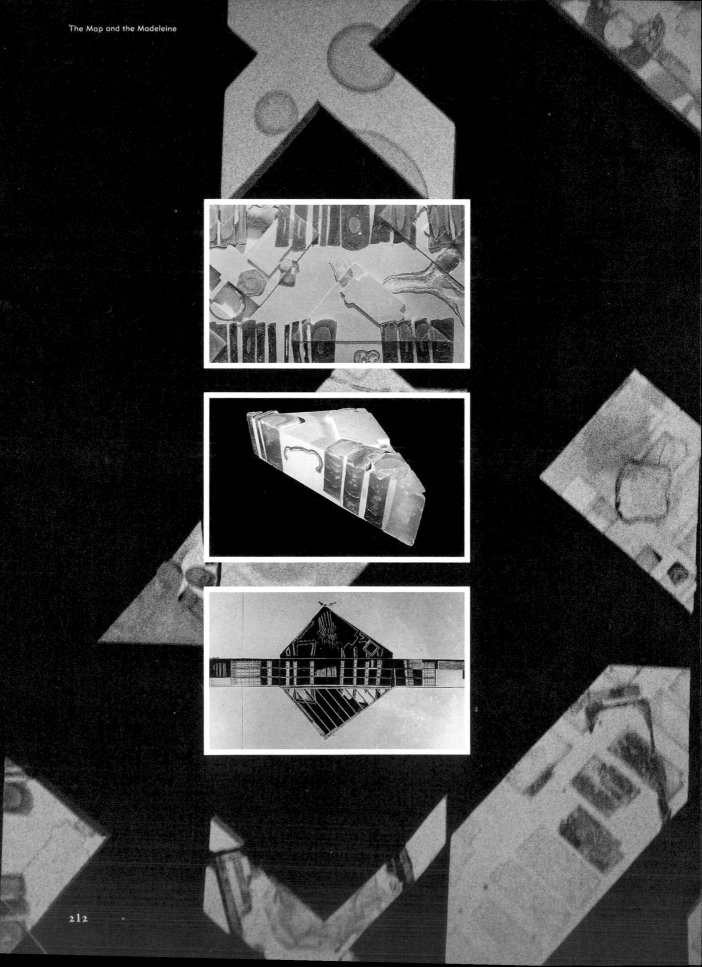

We created a space by juxtaposing the map of Detroit and the collection of household objects. The reading of the map was transformed by intertwining private and public spaces, artifact and map, symbol and index, drawing and model, geometry and memory. The possibilities of interpretation are as many as the number of sections; one moves from one building topology and history to another, from one building structure to another, from one associative memory to another: a repository of forms with no final configuration. This multiplicity reflects the clarifying and obscuring processes used to construct the map, shuttling between rational process and involuntary intuition.

Conclusion

The program evolved under the hypothesis that the reflection of ourselves, our bodies, and our intellectual constructs links all scales of our built world. The Studio searched to understand and isolate similar relationships across the various scales. We may examine a madeleine or a map; in our absence these items speak about ourselves, our limits and possibilities, our constructs of space, culture, and language, and the needs and desires of our bodies.

The inspiration provided by Proust's vision of the potent power of a "banal" object to recall experience and enrich his internal world and by Borges's utopian representation of the world as an absurd full-scale map has challenged us to combine these aspects and constructs of ourselves and our world in our work. The immediate experience of acting and remembering and the distanced experience of mapping and representing are both essential to making architecture.

Notes

1. This is an abridged version of Ronit Eisenbach, "The Map and the Madeleine," *Dimensions 7*, Journal of the School of Architecture and Urban Planning at the University of Michigan (1993), 12–17.

2. Marcel Proust, *Remembrance of Things Past*, vol. 1, *Swann's Way* (New York: Vintage Books, 1981), 51.

3. Samuel Beckett, *Proust* (New York: Grove Press, 1981), 21.

4. Jorge Luis Borges, "Of Exactitude in Science," in *A Universal History of Infamy* (New York: Dutton, 1972), 141.

Ariadne's Thread / Rumi's Ocean[1]

September 1992–May 1993

If you wish to outline an architecture which conforms to the structure of our soul . . . it would have to be conceived in the image of the labyrinth.

—Nietzsche, *Aurore*[2]

If Descartes did not know how to get through the labyrinth, it was because he sought its secret of continuity in rectilinear tracks, and the secret of liberty in a rectitude of the soul. He knew the inclension of the soul as little as he did the curvature of matter. A "cryptographer" is needed, someone who can at once account for nature and decipher the soul, who can peer into the crannies of matter and read into the folds of the soul.

—Gilles Deleuze, *The Fold: Leibniz and the Baroque*

Work by Manuel Báez

The unity that Deleuze demands between matter and soul is the Orphic unity of the pre-Socratics, Lucretius, Ovid, and the metaphysical tradition—the unity whose split begins with the modern scientific approach emerging during the Renaissance and culminating in Descartes. The quintessential Renaissance artist-architect Leonardo da Vinci rejected this new scientific method of inquiry in the last years of his life. Da Vinci's studies and meditations on vision, the human eye, and such natural phenomena as the dynamics of water and waves led him into an unsuccessful search for new ways of depicting and analyzing the turbulent dynamics of nature and lived experience. Meanwhile, the scientific approach advanced with increasing faith in a mathematical system of laws and in quantitative description and analysis of the physical world. An unprecedented rise in science and technology ensued, establishing the undisputed reign of classical physics. The classical tradition in architecture exemplifies the stability of this vision of order.

The classical ideal of the absolute predictability and uniformity of the world, which required the Cartesian split between matter and soul, was shattered in our century in the arts and in science by Einsteinian relativity, quantum mechanics, and chaos theory. A new paradigm with far-reaching philosophical and aesthetic repercussions has emerged. The geometries and perspectives of absolute determinism function only within a limited domain whose restrictive borders have given way to the turbulent ebb and flow of a swirling, dynamic universe. This is the turbulence upon which da Vinci meditated and that he rendered in exquisite detail. The study of what were assumed to be very simple, classically determinist systems consisting of only a few elements has unveiled systems that will eventually generate chaotic, unpredictable behavior. Order and disorder are inextricably interwoven.

Manuel Báez's work, like that of Deleuze's cryptographer, seeks folds in matter that extend through the soul. In this case, however, the map is in motion, found in the patterns of nonlinear, dynamic complexities. Consistent with the Studio's method, Báez began his investigations with an empirical analysis of a physical phenomenon: the wave action generated by a string attached to a spinning wheel. This generative force spins the string into "attractor" forms that lurk within the unfolding modulations between the mass of the string and the medium of resistance (air friction and gravity). The movement of the whirling string draws lines of force that course through a sinuous architecture of curved space, recalling the dance of Nietzsche's labyrinth and Ariadne's thread.

"Force is a spiritual power, an invisible energy arising from motion," wrote da Vinci in his notebooks.[3] The sensuous lines in these moving folds are generated by elemental conditions of nature and therefore resonate with the innate structure of our embodied consciousness. Their sinuous flow embodies the cosmic forces that are the subject of the mystical tradition, expressed in the oceanic rhythms that according to the Sufi poet Rumi reveal the "inclension of the soul" in the corresponding "curvature of matter."

Notes

1. The title of this work, written by Studio participant Manuel Báez, is two-fold. The first part refers to Ariadne, the mythological Greek guide to the labyrinth, which itself symbolizes chaos and the individual life. One follows her unwinding ball of thread to get through the labyrinth. The second part refers to Jalai al-Din Rumi, the great Persian mystic poet of the thirteenth century and the creator of the whirling, circular dance of the Mevlevi dervishes.

2. As quoted in Jay Fellows, *Ruskin's Maze: Mystery and Madness in His Art* (Princeton: Princeton University Press, 1981), 1.

3. Leonardo da Vinci, *The Notebooks of Leonardo da Vinci: A Memorial Edition* (New York: Raynal, 1956), 62.

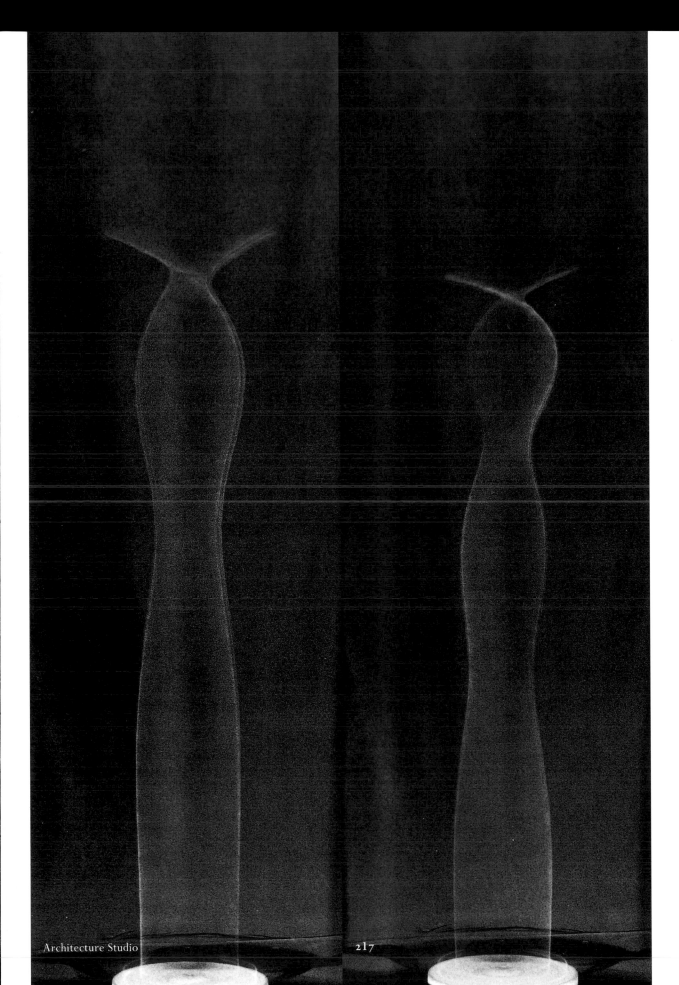

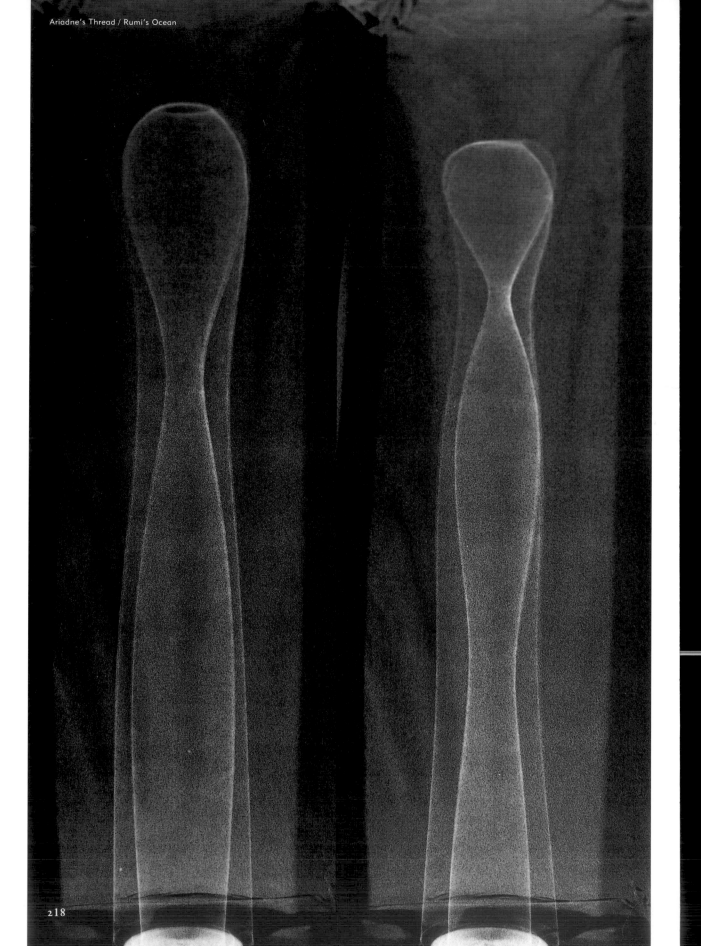

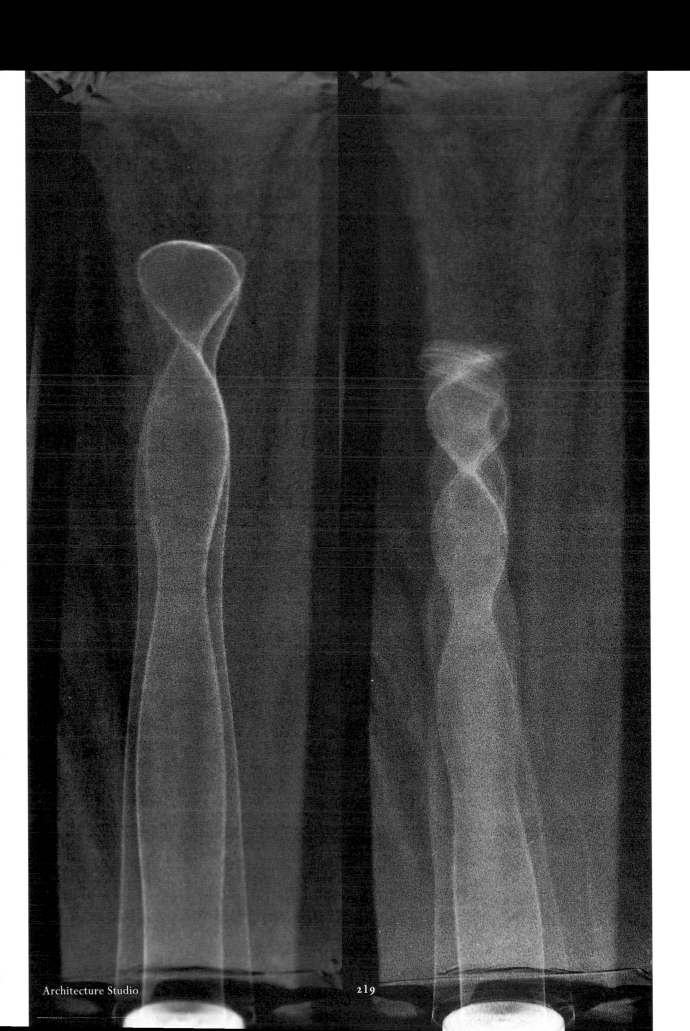